ON PSYCHOLOGICAL
LANGUAGE

INTERNATIONAL LIBRARY OF PSYCHOLOGY

ON PSYCHOLOGICAL LANGUAGE

and the Physiomorphic Basis of Human Nature

GRAHAM RICHARDS

ROUTLEDGE
London and New York

First published 1989
by Routledge
11 New Fetter Lane, London EC4P 4EE

Simultaneously published in the USA and Canada
by Routledge, a division of Routledge, Chapman and Hall, Inc.
29 West 35th Street, New York, NY 10001

Laserset by LaserScript Ltd, Mitcham, Surrey
Printed and bound in Great Britain by
Biddles Ltd, Guildford and King's Lynn

British Library Cataloguing in Publication Data
Richards Graham
On psychological language and the physiomorphic basis
of human nature.
I. Title
150

Library of Congress Cataloging in Publication Data
Richards, Graham.
On psychological language and the physiomorphic basis
of human nature/by Graham Richards.
p. cm.
Bibliography: p.
Includes index.
1. Psychology–Terminology. 2. Onomasiology. I. Title.
BF32.R5 1989
150'14–dc20
89-6321
CIP

ISBN 0-415-01038-1 9_ 10-90

TO MAURA

AND IN MEMORY OF OUR DEAR NEPHEW
LIAM COLLINS
1957–1989

'. . . one with the man in the wind
and the west moon'

Dylan Thomas

whenever we *Attempt* to frame any *Ideas,* properly speaking, of the Mind's Operations or the *Manner* of them, they prove no more than *Indirect Metaphorical Images* borrowed from Sense and Imagination; and no *Direct Representations* or *Original Ideas* of anything transacted in the Mind it self. What a large Stock of Ideas and Words for that purpose doth the Eye with its Objects furnish to Speech ? This being the noblest and most extensive Organ of Sensation, and its Objects most plain and delightful, we choose the Words belonging to it, to express most of the Operations of the Eye of the Mind; and when these fail, we have recourse to the rest of our Senses. *Perception* is a Word and Idea transfered from the View and Sight we take of *Material* Objects, to a quality of the pure Intellect. *Discerning* is supposed to be something in the Mind like a Power the *Eye* hath of distinguishing its different Objects. So *Comparing* Ideas takes its rise from a nice and particular View of two or more *Visible* Objects at the same Time.

Bishop Peter Browne (1733) *Things Divine and Supernatural Conceived by Analogy with Things Natural and Human*

As by the cultivation of various sciences, a language is amplified, it will be more furnished with words deflected from their original sense; the geometrician will talk of a courtier's zenith, or the eccentrick virtue of a wild hero, and the physician of sanguine expectations and phlegmatick delays.

Dr Johnson (1755) *Preface* to
Dictionary of the English Language.

Since the analogies are rot
Our senses based belief upon
We have no means of learning what
Is really going on

W.H. Auden (1958) *Friday's Child*

CONTENTS

PREFACE

This book is intended as a fairly formal, even schematic, statement of a Psychological theory on which I have been ruminating for many years. Although it focuses initially on language, it has serious implications for the way in which we view human evolution itself, implications which are sketched out in Chapters 5 and 6. I am now uncertain quite how the underlying idea originated, although I do recall thinking, sometime around 1970, that there was something odd about saying that it was anthropomorphic to call a sheep 'sheepish'. The term 'physiomorphism' around which the theory hinges was culled from Lévi-Strauss, as explained in the text. I am still not entirely happy with it and even having completed the book I am acutely aware that the concept needs considerable refinement (see Appendix B). The rudiments of the argument of the present work as it pertains to human evolution were briefly smuggled into Richards (1987b) and more fully discussed in Richards (1989). The function of this work is primarily to introduce the basic structure of the theory into the public arena for critical collective evaluation.

In developing this theory I have been, in effect, attempting to integrate my three principle areas of interest: the nature of psychological language, the history of Psychology, and human evolution. This may seem to be a far-flung triad, but I hope it will be demonstrated that they can be brought into productive juxtaposition with one another.

In order to keep this account as concise as possible I have not, in some places at any rate, referenced it as fully as some might wish. I should perhaps reassure them that I am aware that many of the issues discussed connect to other contemporary debates (particularly on such matters as metaphor, discourse analysis, and hermeneutics), while others are central concerns of modern anthropology. It is, though, difficult in the present academic climate to retain one's intellectual autonomy; to reconcile the conflicting demands of engaging in ongoing traditions of discourse and working through one's ideas independently. However, a satisfying integration of the latter with the former can surely best be achieved only after one has clarified them to the best of one's ability. The 'invisible college' has nonetheless been consulted and I would like to express gratitude to the following for their interest, comments, and criticisms (which I have sought to address): Phil Evans, Dean Falk, Jim Good, David Knight, Robert Lowe, Mary Midgley, Marian Pitts, Roy Porter, Arthur Still, Chris Stringer, Elizabeth Valentine, and Max Velmans. I would also like to thank Clive Gabriel for fitting the second drive in my Amstrad (since when the task of completing this book has been eased considerably), and Sabrina Izzard for maintaining my second-hand book supplies. And, of course, without Maura's support and love this would undoubtedly have fizzled out like a dozen previous efforts. Any faults are, alas, solely my own responsibility.

Tunbridge Wells, September 1989

INTRODUCTION: THE ANTHROPOMORPHIC ILLUSION

Misleading beliefs may, over time, acquire uncritical universal acceptance not from any weight of favourable evidence but because their superficial plausibility has rendered them immune to re-examination. Only when the ramifications of their eventual overthrow come to be explored do their stultifying effects become apparent. That heavy objects fall more quickly than light ones, that planets move in perfect circular orbits, that Time is absolute, that the Moon is unreachable, and that a witness's degree of certainty reflects the likelihood of his or her recall being correct are examples of such beliefs, all now known to be false. This book begins by reappraising another such belief, still widely and routinely accepted – the belief that our primitive ancestors in some way projected human characteristics onto the natural world, that they viewed the cosmos 'anthropomorphically'. This myth of primitive anthropomorphism has, it is true, not gone entirely unchallenged, particularly by the French anthropologist Lévi-Strauss (1972), but his challenge occured in the generally inaccessible context of structuralist theorizing and had little influence beyond anthropology itself, even in France where Jacques Monod routinely repeated the myth in his highly acclaimed book *Chance and Necessity* (1972).[1] That the myth is no respecter of ideological position is evidenced by its equally routine reiteration in Govinda's *The Psychological Attitude of Early Buddhist Philosophy* (1961).

The case against the primitive anthropomorphism myth, and an alternative 'physiomorphic' account, are given in Chapter 1, and the balance of the book explores some of the consequences of replacing it with the latter. These consequences extend in a

1

number of directions not usually associated in academic literature, such as human evolution studies, history of religion, and the psychology of personality. In pursuing these implications it became apparent that certain very basic issues required some degree of rethinking, specifically: the nature of linguistic communication, the roots of human behavioural diversity, and the psychological background of the current crisis in human affairs. Not all of this required rethinking is revolutionary, but it does seem to entail serious modifications to currently prevailing formulae.

Before launching into these deeper waters it is worth considering why the primitive anthropomorphism myth has endured for so long. It came to the fore, of course, during the early nineteenth-century, for example in Comte's positivism, with the introduction of evolutionary (albeit pre-Darwinian) perspectives into the Western intellectual arena. The broad consensus was that science represented the highest form of thought, and that it had evolved from earlier modes of thought of a cruder, less rational, and more infantile kind. To nineteenth-century Europeans these modes of thought seemed to be exemplified in the animistic belief systems of the tribal subjects of their colonial empires, the irrationality of which they saw as self-evident. The need for science to contrast itself with an inferior pre-science coincided with the need of imperial rulers to contrast themselves with their colonial subjects in a fashion which legitimized their master–subject relationship (see Kuper 1988 for a full account of the development and persistence of the very notion of 'primitive society'). Anthropomorphism was not, however, considered to be the monopoly of the savage or unscientific. In the wake of Darwin the study of animal behaviour attracted increasing attention, and the more rigorously scientific of its students became scornful of the manner in which the subject had hitherto been tackled. There can be little doubt that Victorian sentimentality produced anthropomorphic works on animal behaviour of a quite extreme kind, such as Lauder Lindsay's *Mind in the Lower Animals* (1880), with its sections on canine suicides, ornithological criminality, feline sulky indignation and the like. In 1894 Lloyd Morgan formulated his famous 'Canon'[2] which was soon taken as representing the formal rejection of anthropomorphism from animal behaviour studies (Lloyd Morgan 1894, 1900). A more

Cartesian attitude to animals as complex machines re-established itself in science as true rationality. Thus positivist science, imperialist ideology, and animal behaviour research were in accord that something called anthropomorphism was a) erroneous and b) typical of unscientific thought. Under the circumstances few would be inclined to query such a belief, serving as it did to bolster both Science and Empire.

But what was anthropomorphism? Here we are on more difficult ground, and although a fuller account of the complexities of the issue will be given in due course, we can note one immediate difficulty. If the error is a simple one and easily avoided there must be prior certainty as to which properties are uniquely human and which are not. Lloyd Morgan's phrase 'lower in the psychological scale' implies that we already know what this scale is. In fact, of course, the whole thrust of Darwin's *Descent of Man* (1871) was to challenge precisely this assumption; the animal penetrated into the human and the human into the animal; the border was blurred; Man still bore within him 'the indelible stamp of his lowly origin' (1874:947). Whilst we might not quibble with labelling as anthropomorphic the ascription of jealousy to limpets (except in a poetic context – one could pen a line like 'the limpet envying the rock's superior immobility'), higher mammals are a different matter. The notion that anthropomorphism was an obvious and readily avoided pitfall unfortunately received reinforcement from the adoption of operational, positivist concepts of science by animal psychologists in the early years of this century (notably Watson's Behaviorism). Here good scientific method itself seemed to require the abandonment of all 'mentalistic' concepts. Once animals had been denied consciousness they were of course denied any psychological properties at all.

The logical conclusion, and one which some (e.g. A. P. Weiss 1925) were ready to draw, was that this applied even to the study of human behaviour and that it was in a sense an 'anthropomorphic' error even to ascribe psychological properties to humans! This was often presented as a bold rejection of Cartesian mind–body dualism and fuzzy metaphysics. Recent years have seen a return to sense over this; interest in the evolution of behaviour has revived and the human–animal borderline returned as a genuine issue (e.g. Stephen Walker 1983), not one to be artificially resolved by methodological fiat. Philosophers (e.g. M. Midgley 1979) have savaged the positivist position on the issue (pointing out that our grounds for ascribing mental states to animals are precisely the same ones we use for ascribing them to humans), and concern with animal welfare has risen in the West to unprecedented heights. Anthropomorphism, then, is not a self-evident error; it is true that we ought not to ascribe uniquely human properties to non-humans inappropriately, or properties unique to one kingdom, phylum, family, genus, or species to another, but the identification of which properties are so unique is itself very much the point at issue.

Difficulty arises also in the matter of ascription of anthropomorphic projection to ancient human cultures or current tribal ones. There is a sort of linguistic illusion in play here. Very few people actually know the original languages in which the beliefs of such cultures are, or were, couched, and nobody does at all in the case of prehistoric cultures. Where these beliefs are known it is primarily via translations into modern European languages. But if the language in question does not or did not make a distinction between animacy and inanimacy (as a key example) any translation into a modern European tongue will invariably give the impression that the culture was incorrectly applying one of them. In other words, there is a tendency to convict such cultures of confusing concepts which they do or did not actually possess. Anthropologists have long been conscious of this problem; W. H. R. Rivers noted it in a paper published in 1926 (Rivers 1926) with regard to the inappropriateness of translating the Melanesian terms *mate* and *to a* by *death* and *life* respectively and Evans-Pritchard wrote;

> What may appear to be hopeless contradictions when
> translated into English may not appear so in the native
> language. When, for instance, a native statement is translated
> that a man of such-and-such a clan is a leopard, it appears to
> us to be absurd, but the word he uses which we translate by
> "is" may not have the same meaning for him that the word "is"
> has for us.

(1981:129)

I will return to this in more detail later in the work but one example might suffice here. Suppose there was originally a single omnibus concept which meant 'coming into being', a concept

4

applied to everything from childbirth to plants sprouting, the new Moon, dawn, and cosmic origins. The temptation here would be to construe all such accounts as anthropomorphic applications of the childbirth concept, rather than seeing that our current ability to identify many varieties of genetic process results from centuries of conceptual differentiation *out of* the original, general, concept (and of course we continue to use the word 'birth' to talk about the births of suns, ideas, political institutions, and nations).

In short, we should not accuse people of misapplying concepts they may not have. Accusations of anthropomorphism often stem from this error, particularly in relation to the concepts of animacy and inanimacy. Failure to deploy this distinction in a way congruent with our own is not anthropomorphism, even if a distinction apparently translatable into these terms exists in the source culture. Our own current demarcation line has only been achieved after centuries of analysis and exploration, during which organic explanations for e.g. the generation of minerals in the *bowels* of the earth were empirically discovered to be false – and likewise purely chemical explanations for 'fermentation'[3]. These discoveries did not occur because researchers had a clearer idea of the difference between animate and inanimate but rather the reverse. It was the discoveries which clarified, or furthered research into, the difference. Below a certain level of empirical knowledge it is simply not clear what criteria can be used to make the distinction and hence it is made crudely or not at all, and the world experienced in different terms altogether. Why are fire, water, and the wind not animate? And why are lichens, pollen, and coral not inanimate?

Another preliminary point to be stressed is that anthropomorphism and anthropocentrism are not synonymous – indeed they are to some extent opposites. This is important because alongside the notion of primitive anthropomorphism exists an equally nigh-on-universally accepted notion of primitive anthropocentrism. What is overlooked is that if one peoples the universe in anthropomorphic fashion with autonomous human-like powers and forces, and especially if these are seen as controlling human affairs in some way, this is not anthropocentric at all. It requires all kinds of propitiations, pleadings, prayers, sacrifices, and compromises with human self-interest to survive in this community of beings. The anthropocentric position is quite different, and best exemplified in modern Western industrial cultures where the entire planetary geosphere, biosphere, atmosphere, and beyond has been viewed as properly subjugated to human self-interest (everything is a 'resource'). In a sense, science itself has been a foremost factor in producing this anthropocentric 'conquest of Nature', though the Judaeo–Christian Genesis story prepared the ground for it in depicting Adam as having dominion over beasts and plants, these being provided by God for human use. The relationship between the two concepts is more complex than this, as we will see in due course, and although neither eventually proves adequate for characterizing 'primitive' thought, it is necessary to draw attention to the fallacy involved in eliding them.

What has all this to do with psychological language? Without pre-empting the fuller discussion to come, the initial theoretical riddle regarding psychological language is to explain how it can be generated in the first place, given the subjectivity of the phenomena to which it refers. This is problematical since the meaning of words originates in, and is sustained by, collectively agreed rules as to their correct use; thus the denotational meaning of a word requires a publicly accessible class of referents. In the case of psychological language no such class exists, by definition. If we accept the primitive anthropomorphism myth, however, we are obliged to assume that psychological properties and phenomena were identified and labelled prior to their 'projection' onto the public, external, world. If, as the linguistic argument just cited suggests, this is impossible, then the primitive anthro-pomorphism myth collapses. To quote Lévi-Strauss:

but how could he have done this [anthropomorphic pro-jection] without simultaneously making the opposite move of attributing a power and efficacy comparable to that of natural phenomena to his own actions? This man, externalized by man, can serve to shape a god only if the forces of nature have already been internalized in him. The mistake made by Comte and the majority of his successors was to believe that man could at all plausibly have peopled nature with wills com-parable to his own without ascribing some of the attributes of this nature, in which he detected himself, to his desires

(1966:220)

Later he coins the term 'physiomorphism' for this opposite process, a term I have adopted. As already mentioned the implications of this insight have so far failed to percolate beyond anthropology (if even there).

The first two chapters which follow seek to spell out a theoretical position regarding psychological language in general. In Chapters 3 and 4 I explore in more detail the implications of this for everyday psychological language and the language of Psychology, the discipline (capitalized to disambiguate from the subject-matter sense – see Richards 1987)[4]. In Chapter 5 the implications for human psychological evolution are outlined. These are among the most fundamental consequences of the physiomorphic theory, since it will be shown that these carry beyond the purely linguistic realm to the nature of human learning itself. Finally I have attempted to spell out, if somewhat briefly, the overall picture of the current human situation which emerges from this. This may seem a grandiose aim, but one justification for academic work of this kind at the present historical juncture is that it sheds some light in this direction, or at least tries to.

CHAPTER ONE

THE 'PHYSIOMORPHIC THEORY' OF PSYCHOLOGICAL LANGUAGE

INTRODUCTION

In the light of subsequent complexities only a provisional, very general definition of what is meant by 'psychological language' will be given here. By 'psychological language' is meant, simply, the use of language to refer to psychological events, states, and phenomena. This ranges from synonyms and near-synonyms for the 'psychological' realm itself (such as *mind, consciousness, thought,* and *psyche*) through psychological state-terms (*worried, confused, happy, curious*), supposed psychological faculties (*intelligence, memory, will*), personality descriptors (*extraverted, stupid, lazy, cheerful*), and interpersonal behaviour (*to warn, to fascinate, to frighten*) to technical terms used by Psychology (*repressed, equilibration, n.Ach., loosened construing, disthymic*). Although psychological language use is not just a matter of vocabulary, (concepts may be encoded in proverbs and fables for example) this level does provide the obvious and easiest starting point for any analysis of its character. It is also important to stress, of course, that not all psychological communication is conducted via psychological language.

Before proceeding further it is worthwhile reminding ourselves of two important features of psychological language (henceforth: PL). Firstly, a large number of its concepts have a quite fluid syntactic status, being commonly used in noun, verb, adjectival and/or adverbial forms (*thought, to think, thoughtful, thoughtfully / intelligence, intelligent, intelligently / worry, to worry, worried, worrying*). It is not unique in this respect (cf. *rain, to rain, rainy*); English syntax itself ensures indeed, in principle, that 'all nouns can be verbed' (although with many natural object terms such a move would be decidedly odd, for example *to river*; but even here one should not underestimate the possibilities – I could imagine only too well hearing a US spokesman saying that 'recent rainfall has riverized the entire region'). It is the fact that these terms actually *are* so generally 'verbed' (and adjectived and adverbed too) which is significant, for it points to a genuine uncertainty as to whether psychological phenomena are to be considered as things, properties, or processes. This has caused perennial problems to Psychology, as the current state–trait controversy in personality theory illustrates; (Mischel 1973 being a *locus classicus* for this). Secondly, even within the PL realm, the same term can be used to refer to phenomena of more than one level: I not only see how to get somewhere, I also see what you're getting at; I can feel pain, but also I can feel afraid, uncertain, and that it's time to go. Ryle, in *The Concept of Mind* (1949) cleverly exploited both of these features in an effort to untangle the Mind–Body problem. We will see in due course the extent to which his solution holds water, although I intend tackling the Mind–Body problem only in a somewhat oblique manner.

HOW THE PROBLEM ARISES

We can now move on to the central problem. PL refers either to phenomena which are publicly inaccessible for direct inspection (as when I report on my thought processes) or to a dimension of public phenomena which is similarly so (as when I accuse you of *deliberately* hitting me, or describe a facial expression as a *welcoming smile*). In the latter case one is often ascribing motives or diagnosing psychological states which underlie overt public behaviour. Perhaps the majority of our behaviour terms are of this kind (we rarely merely refer to physical movements *per se*: people are *doing* something). In the case of language itself, verbal behaviour, Austin (1962) claimed this was always the case. One is always informing, advising, warning, congratulating, ordering, apologizing, amusing, etc. over and above the specific content of the message. He refers to this as the 'illocutionary force' of an utterance, a topic to which we return in the next chapter. For the moment the feature of PL which concerns us is the apparent privacy of its referents, existing as they do in the 'minds' of the PL-users, beyond the range of public denotation.

Wittgenstein's *Philosophical Investigations* (1953) is an enigmatic work to say the least. It is concerned primarily with disclosing the misleading nature of many of our assumptions about the nature of language and meaning, and how these lie at the heart of traditional philosophical problems. Among these disclosures are two of immediate relevance: a) his demonstration that meaning is a collective product of the language-using community, continually being renegotiated, and sustained by publicly agreed rules as to correct usage, including denotational rules (although 'denotation' itself cannot be denotationally defined); b) his argument against the possibility of a private language, which derives from a) since meanings of words in a language which I invent and of which I am the sole speaker, cannot be sustained; defining such words is akin, to use Wittgenstein's metaphor, to my left hand giving my right hand a cheque. (The key paragraphs in *Philosophical Investigations* are nos. 268–75.) The argument against private language has been mulled over at length by philosophers since Wittgenstein introduced it, but its validity in the particular case of a private language to refer to what is private, or subjective, has, I believe, to be accepted. With no other witness than myself there is no way that the subjective experience I use to define 'X' at time t_1 can be compared to that occurring at t_2. 'X' is superfluous, neither helping nor hindering the accuracy of my recall, since a 'mistaken' use of 'X' can never be known. (In fact the impossibility is not at heart a matter of unverifiable memory, but, as Gert (1986) shows, hinges on the incoherence of the definition process itself under these circumstances.) When closely scrutinized the very notion of a private language turns out to be fundamentally paradoxical, while it is impossible to conceive of any function such an invention could usefully serve.

Given that PL is used to refer to essentially private phenomena, and given the broad validity of the Wittgensteinian accounts of meaning and the impossibility of directly defining word-meanings in terms of private events, the question clearly arises as to how PL is possible at all. How can it be possible to sustain the meanings of the terms which comprise the basis of PL in the absence of public criteria for defining their correct usage? Surprisingly this is a topic to which virtually no attention has been paid, although the range of PL vocabulary was investigated by Allport and Odbert (1936) and its use in personality description entertainingly researched by Bromley in *Personality Description in Ordinary Language* (1977). The work which comes nearest to anticipating the position advocated here comes not from Psychology but from the linguistics– philosophy borderline, namely Lakoff and Johnson's *Metaphors We Live By* (1980); these authors however are so fascinated by exploring the metaphors themselves that they fail to appreciate the theoretical significance of the situation they are describing. The reason for this widespread neglect lies perhaps in the tendency of philosophers in the wake of logical positivism to seek a solution, as Ryle did, by demonstrating that PL did not refer to a private domain anyway but was ultimately about overt behaviour, echoing Behaviorism at a more (far more) sophisticated level. Philosophical disdain for the problem of consciousness, to some extent fuelled by the initial reading of *Philosophical Investigations*, meant that the PL problem remained largely unexamined. Psychologists could remain content that contemporary philosophers had logically demonstrated that all PL was covert behaviour-language, and the philosophers could remain content that they had demonstrated that there was no problem in any case. The principal exception to this was Austin, who died prematurely in 1960; even so, the debates he initiated have remained by and large in the province of philosophy (e.g. Searle 1969; Ninio 1986), infiltrating only slowly into Psychology (e.g. Winograd 1980).

THE PHYSIOMORPHIC MODEL

The obvious route to take to see how vocabulary is generated is via etymology. Here we are up against a further irony: the heyday of etymological investigation was the nineteenth century, when philology and linguistics were conceived as concerned with little else. It was this, they believed, which would disclose the relationships between languages and their evolution, and via that gain a glimpse into prehistoric movements of people and ideas (see R. H. Robins 1967, Ch. 7, and G. Sampson 1980, Ch. 1). Max Müller even identified the twenty fundamental concepts from which he held all subsequent ideas to have proceeded. Baron Bunsen (*not* the inventor of the bunsen burner) calculated, on the

11

basis of rate of language divergence from a common origin, that the human race was at least 20,000 years old.[1] The study of etymology would in fact reveal the very nature of human thought itself, as the title of Müller's *The Science of Thought* (1887) made explicit. Around the turn of the century this evolutionary, 'diachronic' approach to language was challenged by the 'synchronic', 'structuralist' linguistics of De Saussure (1916) which gave priority to quite different issues. Modern linguistic theories of whatever school rarely appear seriously interested in the prosaic topic of etymology. This is not to say that nobody is interested in etymology any more, but that experts in this field no longer see themselves as playing a central role in addressing such weighty issues as the nature of thought and certainly seem to have ceased writing books on such topics. Etymology is a treacherous area for the untrained to enter but while first mooting the 'physiomorphic' idea some years ago I encountered with some shock the following passage in William Dwight Whitney's *The Life and Growth of Language*:

> A conspicuous branch of the department of figurative transfer, and one of indispensable importance in the history of language, is the application of terms having a physical, sensible meaning, to the designation of intellectual and moral conceptions and their relations. It is almost useless to attempt to illustrate this; the examples would come crowding in too numerously to be dealt with: we will merely notice a few of those which happen to be offered in the preceding (*sic*) paragraph. *Perplex* means 'braid together, intertwine.' *Simple* is 'without fold,' as distinguished from what is *double* or 'two-fold;' in *simplicity* and *duplicity* we have a moral contrast more distinctly brought to view; *application* contains the same root, and denotes an actual physical 'folding or bending to' any-thing, so as to fit it closely; while *imply* intimates a 'folding in.'
>
> (1876:88)

He continues with further examples for a page before concluding

> In fact, our whole mental and moral vocabulary has been gained precisely in this way; the etymologist feels that he has not finished tracing out the history of any one of its terms

12

until he has hunted it back to the physical conception in
which, by the general analogies of language, it must have had
its origin.

(1876:89)

Whitney, Professor of Sanskrit and Comparative Philology at Yale,
was one of the most eminent of nineteenth-century linguists, cited
with approval by De Saussure himself (particularly as one who saw
language as existing at the level of communal practice, rather than
as a transpersonal entity). His tone certainly suggests that it was
common knowledge among members of his profession that what I
am terming PL was generated by 'figurative transfer' from terms
referring to the physical world. This was reiterated by Moncalm
(1905) in a slightly different way: 'The source of all abstract ideas
lies in acts which are entirely material' (1905:91). Whitney and
Müller, though they engaged in a long controversy regarding the
fundamental nature of language, and particularly on whether
linguistics was to be considered a historical (Whitney) or a physical
(Müller) science, were in accord at least on this particular issue.
The difficulties such an account raises for the primitive
anthropomorphism myth seem rarely to have been recognized.
The Danish psychologist Höffding (1891) is one of the exceptions,
noting not only that all psychological terms originated in physical
world terms (a view he ascribes to both Locke and Leibniz) but
also observing of the 'mythological theory' which 'attributes to
primitive man a tendency to conceive and explain all natural
phenomena by everywhere introducing his own conscious life':

And were the theory correct, it would necessarily be expected
that language would denote material things by terms
originally applied to mental things, whereas in reality it
denotes mental things by terms originally material.

(1891:7)

An obvious initial hypothesis, therefore, is that PL is generated by
the reflexive application of what I will term 'World Language'
(WL). This outflanks the philosophical difficulties by anchoring
word meanings in the public arena. In order to refer to the
subjective, what I am at heart doing is saying 'I/you/she/he/they

13

am/is/are like X' where X is a public phenomenon (or '...am/is/are X-ing, X-y, X-ish' where X is a public process or quality).

ZEN, SCHRÖDINGER AND MIRANDOLA

The implications of this are more far-reaching than we might initially appreciate, but meanwhile here is a traditional Zen (actually Ch'an, being Chinese) anecdote:

> In his bid for the Sixth Patriarchy of the Tung Ch'an monastery, Shen Hsiu, the leading contender, responded to the Fifth Patriarch's test of a stanza on the Essence of Mind by writing on the wall:
>
> > Our body is the Bodhi-tree
> > And our mind a mirror bright
> > Carefully we wipe them hour by hour
> > And let no dust alight.
>
> The illiterate Hui Neng (638–713), a novice on rice-pounding duty, on getting this read out to him dictated the following riposte:
>
> > There is no Bodhi-tree
> > Nor stand of mirror bright.
> > Since all is void
> > Where can the dust alight?
>
> which got him the job along with the robe and begging bowl that went with it, (but he had to leave at midnight in a hurry to avoid, it seems, the wrath of the jealous Shen Hsiu and his cronies (see A. F. Price and Wong Mou-lam 1969)).

Mind *per se* is propertyless, a void. This is not mere mystification but a conclusion that was reached from a quite different direction by Erwin Schrödinger, one of this century's greatest physicists, in his 1956 Tarner Lectures (Schrödinger 1967). He talks of the

> curious double role that the conscious mind acquires. On the one hand it is the stage...on which (the) whole world process

14

takes place...outside which there is nothing. On the other hand we gather the impression... that within this world-bustle the conscious mind is tied up with certain very particular organs (brains) which...serve after all only to maintain the lives of their owners.'

(1967:147)

But he continues

'On the one hand mind is the artist who has produced the whole; in the accomplished work, however, it is but an insignificant accessory that might be absent without detracting from the total effect.'

(1967:148).

Mind is thus entirely neutral, an arena in which the universe happens, indeed the creator of that universe insofar as it is known at all, but in itself characterless.

Possessors of minds cannot, though, live on this thought alone. The universe is experienced as divided into subjective and public realms, although the borderline might not be as self-evident as we think. And for humans it is necessary (for reasons which must for the moment be held in abeyance) to be able to communicate about and construe what is going on in the subjective one. One underlying task is perhaps to maintain consensus on where that borderline itself lies, a matter we return to in Chapter 2. All experience is 'in the mind', but which of it is also private? Having demarcated that latter and identified with it as what 'I' actually *am*, I have to be able to linguistically encode the events happening therein to survive as a person in a community of persons. As this encoding can only occur in the way described above, this is tantamount to saying that the psychological is constructed out of the physical, that its qualities and properties are as it were 'introjected' or assimilated to become our own. Put succinctly, there is no such thing as 'Human Nature', only 'Nature' reflexively and selectively assimilated. The situation was described by the Renaissance humanist Pico della Mirandola in his essay *On The Dignity of Man*. Here, in an oft-quoted passage, God tells Adam:

All other things hav a Nature bounded within certain Laws,

15

Thou only art loos from all, and according to thy own
Counsel in the hand of which I have put Thee, mayst chuse
and prescribe what Nature thou wilt to thy self. I have placed
Thee in the Middle of the World, that from thence thou
mayst behold on every side more commodiously evry thing in
thee whole World. We hav made Thee neither heavenly nor
Earthly Neither Mortal nor Immortal, that being the Honored
Former and Framer of thy self, thou mayst shape thy self into
what Nature thy self pleaseth.[2]

The belief that true knowledge and power were only obtainable by
a drawing of the world into oneself was indeed the central feature
of sixteenth-century Hermetic Philosophy (see Frances A. Yates
1964).

A final example of recognition of the derivative nature of PL is
the philosopher F. Waismann's paper 'Language Strata' (in Flew
(ed.) 1953, but first delivered as a lecture in 1946). 'Remember' he
says 'that almost all terms denoting the mental are derived from
words whose primary connotation was sensuous' (1953:13), then
he devotes over two pages to a quite sensitive evocation of the
phenomenology of this. Evidently, then, the notion that the
psychological is derived from the physical, that we can only
construct our 'human nature' from the external one, is not a new
one, but is present, implicitly or explicitly, in sources as diverse as
seventh-century Chinese Buddhism, Renaissance philosophy,
nineteenth-century linguistics, linguistic philosophy, and modern
French anthropology (not to mention such eighteenth-century
figures as Bishop Browne and Samuel Johnson – see preliminary
quotes).

OBJECTIONS

This initial solution to the PL problem, that PL is generated by
reflexive application of WL, thus has a strong *prima facie*
plausibility, and, if true, apparently reflects an underlying
physiomorphic process by which external world properties
become internalized as psychological ones. Before moving on to
the limitations of this simple version of the model it is necessary to
tackle an important potential objection: in actual fact a large

number of PL terms are not after all metaphorical or figurative in character; how then is their meaning sustained?

It is no part of the physiomorphic thesis that the figurative character of a PL term necessarily be currently apparent. The way word-meanings are learned is not the same as the way word-meanings are generated. In particular the denotational definition procedure, pointing at a public something as a defining instance of the class of referents for which a word X will be used, plays a smaller role in the child's language acquisition than many imagine. The present thesis is about how PL words are generated and sustained, not about how they are learned. Absence of any apparently figurative character in a current PL word should, though, affect its sustainability as a meaningful term. As it turns out such non-figurative terms are rule-proving exceptions, for it is precisely the most abstract and non-figurative PL terms, often very basic ones in our vocabulary, which are accompanied by the greatest number of metaphorical synonyms or amplifiers. The word *sad* for instance (for which a non-PL root is in fact traceable, see Appendix A) exists at the focal point of a vast array of more clearly figurative expressions: *depressed, down in the dumps, low, fed up, pissed off, gloomy, down in the mouth, lousy,* and so forth (some further synonyms: *wretched, miserable, despondent,* for example, are also traceable to terms which are either non-PL or not exclusively PL). The difficulty of defining *love* is almost a paradigm illustrative case of the PL-problem. How does one know one is really in love, that one is subject to this allegedly most important and salient of all subjective experiences? Again a host of metaphoric expressions form a sort of aura around the abstract term, which is sustained as their common focus. But the fluidity of the term in this case is extreme; the privacy of its referent, plus its importance, renders accuracy of identification vital. We are thus forced to consider whether we are not experiencing something similar to, but crucially distinct from, this *love* – infatuation, or lust, or pity, or awe.

The notorious difficulties that making such discriminations presents to us illustrate precisely how *un*self-evident the identification of our inner, psychological states is, and how dependent we are on PL for construing them at all. Other non-figurative PL terms share with *sad* and *love* both a dependency on figurative synonyms to sustain them, and a similar, if less intense, lack of self-evident meaning in the absence of these. The answer to the objection then is twofold: a) current lack of figurative character does not disprove the argument that a term originated by 'figurative transfer', since language acquisition is a different process from word-generation; b) the most important such non-figurative PL terms are in fact sustainable only because they serve as the focus for other terms, synonymous or partially so, which are figurative. (In Appendix A I have listed over seventy apparently non-figurative PL terms with their etymologies. It will be seen there that, apart from a handful of terms mostly of a very general and basic character (e.g. *mind*), they are traceable to roots which are either clearly non-PL, or far more ambiguous in status as PL or WL. The way to disprove the physiomorphic account, however, is not in this direction – failure to trace a WL root does not mean there wasn't one – but in showing a term actually entering PL in some other way, or identifying one for which there are no figurative synonyms or amplifiers.)

A more profound objection may also be raised, that the proposed model implies that all thought is linguistic and that, consequently, its advocacy involves both a hard-line Whorfian position on the language–thought relationship and a denial of thought to non-language-using species. Since both of these have been empirically refuted to most people's satisfaction over the last decade or so, it is essential to clarify how they are reconcilable with the physiomorphic account. Firstly, PL does not itself 'cause' experience or thought; its job is to facilitate the public communication, structuring, and evaluation of experience and thought with a higher degree of specificity than pre-linguistic and non-linguistic modes can achieve. It does this by mapping private, experiential, phenomena onto the public 'world' phenomena. But conversely, since it is very often this public 'world' which is being experienced and thought about in the first place, the structuring and evaluation of the psychological must be done in terms of the WL-encoded structures and values identified in the external world. Now clearly the first PL users inherited a capacity for non-linguistic thought and a species-specific psychology: emotions, ways of reacting to various types of environmental stimuli, certain routine problem-solving strategies, and in all probability a rudimentary self-consciousness (see Suarez and Gallup 1981 on self-awareness in higher primates). Much of this legacy we still possess. Writers such as Stephen Walker (1983) and Adrian Desmond (1979) have convincingly shown that wherever the boundary between thinkers and non-thinkers occurs it is not between humans and higher primates, and may be far further afield. But this existence of psychological 'universals' does not refute the physiomorphic account of PL for two reasons:

(A) Many of these 'universals' are not themselves PL categories but WL categories (e.g. modes of classifying life-forms), only acquiring *psychological* significance following their reflexive use to generate PL categories; they are not, prior to this, psychological properties but apparently in-built (in some sense) ways of classifying world properties. It would be to commit the Psychologist's Fallacy[3] in its basic form to claim that the category 'wug' (worm+bug; see Brown 1979) was itself wug-like. Having made the classification, though, it then becomes possible for us to classify ourselves and others as 'wuggish', creating a PL category. To press the point further, there was no pre-existent human psychological quality of 'wuggishness' being projected onto the outside world even if there was a pre-existent tendency to classify small wriggly creepy creatures together.

(B) Psychologically, the advent of PL does not so much create psychological phenomena such as emotions as objectify them. The pre-linguistic psychological phenomena universally persist but, once subject to PL, they are experienced as entering consciousness or mind rather than constituting it, and become amenable to cultural evaluation etc. The status of emotions prior to their linguistic objectification is simply as global states of the organism with both psychological and behavioural aspects but no reflexive evaluation, no separation of the 'I' who is experiencing the emotion from the emotion itself. One *is* the emotion. By contrast, the PL user is no longer identified with any particular psychological state (though may become 'possessed' by one), but is rather in the position of reflexive onlooker. In short, we can and do have non-linguistic thoughts and cognitions, and we probably share some universal psychological features, but insofar as we can communicate them, discuss them, or evaluate them, we are *at some point* dependent on PL for doing so. I may have a prolonged non-linguistic cognitive reverie in which I plan a painting or a piece of music or rehearse a new motor-skill but ultimately the psychological meaning of this is embedded in the language via which my culture provides the rationales and formal constraints for these behaviours, and indeed the behavioural categories themselves. Much, if not all, of the pertinent language is the PL which encodes the psychological functions of such behaviours as worship, entertainment, judicial procedures, education, or whatever. Whole classes of human behaviour only *exist* at the level of what Wittgenstein called 'language games', insisting that language is 'a form of life'. Many of the subtler emotions may also have only emerged as discriminable nuances of the basic universal emotional states by virtue of PL. (And can there be a 'linguistic emotion' – expressed by the groan that greets a bad pun for example?) The extent of psychological and linguistic universals is an empirical matter, and the answers are as yet incomplete. Psychological phenomena as such are not dependent on the existence of language; if they were, all experience would be linguistic. Classifying, evaluating, analysing, discussing, interrelating, constructing a 'self' out of, and communicating psychological phenomena are, however, so dependent (though some perhaps not exclusively). It is in that sense that the 'psychological' or the 'mind' is to be understood as constructed by PL out of the external world as encoded in WL. And that includes the category 'mind' itself, as will be argued in Chapter 2.

A further, more fundamental reason why the physiomorphic model does not entail a Whorfian position is that the physiomorphic process itself is not an exclusively linguistic one, as we will show at length in due course, but a (perhaps *the*) central human learning strategy, closely related to imitation. The role of language is to control and facilitate it, but the process itself evolved prior to language (see Chapter 5).

A LIMITATION OF THE 'METAPHOR' MODEL

Nevertheless there is a point at which the physiomorphic account in the form so far proposed reaches its limits, and this arises from our uncritical acceptance of the term 'metaphor' (or 'figurative transfer') to describe the process. So far we have depicted the situation as one in which there is a WL used for the public world, from which particular terms are plucked because we identify in the phenomena to which they refer something analogous to, or even identical with, the internal private phenomena which we wish to name. They then become part of PL. Yet when we consider the basic physical property and relational terms which constitute such a substantial portion of our everyday PL, the notion of WL primacy does not seem entirely convincing. Personality-descriptors for example include such terms as *hard/soft, warm/cold, bright/dull, rough/smooth* and *open*. In discussing our thought processes we make use of the whole relational vocabulary so that one can contrive sentences like '*Behind* this idea of his *lay* a *deeper, hidden*, motive – I had *above* all to keep this fact *before* me if I was not to be carried *against* my judgement *beyond* the bounds of common sense'. It strains credibility (though that is not in itself an argument) to believe that, in the first case, the adoption of say *hard* into PL occurred as a sort of poetic witticism in the Upper Palaeolithic, one Cro-Magnon saying to another "You're a very...sort of...*hard*... man" and everybody's eyes lighting up with a shock of recognition at the originality of the metaphor. The italicized words in the second example seem, similarly, so basic to any discourse at all that it is hard to imagine a time in which they were fully deployed in WL but not in PL. These terms were surely Janus-faced from the start. This brings us to the third term between World and Psyche, missing from our discussion so far, the human body.

THE TWO-FACED BODY

The body (as Roy F. Ellen 1977 for example points out)[4] has a dual role as both signifier and signified; that is to say that on the one hand it is via our body that we, as embodied consciousnesses, endow the phenomena of our experience with meaning; on the other, the body itself constitutes one of the phenomena of our experience (indeed, the primary one) requiring meaningful construal. Put another way, the body is both subjective and objective, both the vehicle of consciousness and an object of consciousness. The categories into which the body is classified (which actually vary considerably between different cultures) thus possess a dual character serving as a template for classifying both the external world and the psychological one. Furthermore, and this is crucial, the basic physical properties of the external world are simultaneously known subjectively as properties of the body. These include the properties coded in English by terms such as *hard/soft, warm/cold,* and *rough/smooth* already cited, plus others such as *stiff/limp, solid/hollow, sharp/blunt, wet/dry, bitter/sweet,* and *flexible/rigid.* Only slightly less directly they include other basic sensory phenomena properties such as *loud/quiet/silent,* and *bright/dull.* Relational concepts (*up/down, in/out* etc.), though less obviously physical body terms, may also be included here as originating in our basic physical transactions with the external world.

From the outset then these categories are in both PL and WL realms. They refer to properties of the external world, but they also refer to subjective states – I know what it is to *be* hard for example because bits of my body are hard; hardness is a property of rocks and wood, but also of teeth, knees, fists, and foreheads. As a PL term it cannot then primarily refer only to the physical sensation of hardness but must signify also the state of consciousness accompanying an awareness (particularly in a behavioural context) of my own hardness. But how do we move from this to the more clearly PL usages of the term as personality descriptor and synonym for 'difficult'? The latter I think is relatively unproblematic, deriving fairly straightforwardly from the greater effort needed to work with physically hard materials. The former is more complex: 'being hard' having become part of the psychological repertoire, subsequent learning of its value for the individual and its role in the individual's transactions with the world (including the social world) endows it with *meaning* as a psychological state. The individual exists, however, in a culture in which this meaning has already been ascertained, which may or may not highly value it, which will define the situations and types of person for which it is or is not appropriate (male soldiers or adolescent girls for instance) etc. The 'hard' person is the one who is more-than-usually inclined to utilize that particular mode of relating to the world. Similar analyses could be made of the way other basic sensory property terms have become PL terms to show how their common use in both PL and WL is not a matter of metaphorical transfer, in which one sense is primary, but is rooted in the existentially ambiguous realm of bodily phenomena. (It may be objected that such analyses are purely speculative, and in a sense this is true – the events in question occured too long ago for direct examination. All one can do is call for alternative speculations and evaluate the various plausibilities of our respective accounts as best one can. On the other hand we *are* all actually language-users and as such the very fact that it is these speculations we make, and not others, is itself a kind of evidence in their favour – though I am far from sure what kind of weight to attach to *that* argument!)

This synchronicity of emergence of PL and WL meanings characteristic of basic physical property categories is apparently distinct from the clear-cut 'metaphorical' generation of PL in expressions such as 'he's a real live wire', 'she's gone off the rails', and 'don't play the giddy goat with me!'. The point at which the distinction occurs, though, may be difficult to pin down. Consider the sequence: 'hard', 'inflexible', 'impervious to reason', 'never gives an inch', 'has an almost pathologically rigid ego-defence structure'; it would be wiser to view the situation as one in which there is a continuum between the two, as we move from PL sources in the raw bodily sensation realm to the highly elaborated realms of the natural world itself, social behaviour, and technology. Not that even 'raw bodily sensations' are classified and evaluated homogeneously by all cultures, which results in a considerable cross-cultural variation of what is experienced as 'painful'. Thus in relation to the category 'hard', while on the present argument we would predict it to be in the PL repertoire of all cultures, we would not expect it to have, either as a PL or WL term, a universally identical 'meaning'.

The primary classificatory role of the body raises a further difficulty for the simple version of the physiomorphic model. It has been pointed out above that the body also provides a template for generating classificatory categories for the external world. Examples are not hard to find: rivers have mouths, mountains have feet, trees have limbs, books have spines, there are heads of celery and eyes in needles, and dawn has rosy fingers. In classifying animal body-parts the same terms may be used as for human body-parts even if they correspond to them only tenuously from an anatomical point of view (e.g. the arms of a star-fish). [It must be noted, though, that the reverse also occurs: *muscle* derives from Latin *musculus* = little mouse; part of our leg is known as the calf; and feet of both sexes have balls (as well as this being used for testes and the eye); Brown and Witkowski (1981) in a cross-cultural survey of figurative terms for body parts cite many other examples: the pupil of the eye (itself an example of a widespread use of the 'little person' image – others include 'infant ghost' and 'doll of the eye') is widely termed the 'seed of the eye'; in Zapotec the biceps are the 'toad of the arm', in Spanish 'the lizard', and in Huastec 'the rabbit'; while many English speakers learned to equate their toes with little piggies.] Ellen (1977) provides examples of cultures where the layout of villages and architectural design are planned to correspond to the structure of the body and the parts named accordingly. Surely such evidence points to the kind of fundamental anthropomorphic projection which the physio-morphic theory denies? This may be answered at one level by reasserting the ambiguous status of the body. Applying body-part terms to the external world is not the same as ascribing human psychological properties to it, which is what the anthropomorphic position is understood to mean. Nevertheless there is a challenging issue here which has not yet been touched on, and which Ellen discusses at length, coming, I believe, to an erroneous conclusion. This is the relationship between analytic and synthetic classification.

ANALYTIC AND SYNTHETIC CLASSIFICATION

There are two basic ways in which classification proceeds: analytic and synthetic. Analytic classification refers to 'whole-part' classification, the analysis of something into its components; thus in English we analyse the body into various parts: head, neck, trunk, limbs, genitals, hands, feet, etc., further analysing the head into face, scalp, and ears, and the face into nose, mouth, chin, and so on. Synthetic classification refers to categories of things presumed to have something in common, the classes of phenomena of which our world is comprised; again, in English (but not in all cultures), we class life-forms into plants, animals, and fungi, animals into insects, crustacea, arthropods, reptiles, mammals, birds, etc. Some such classes may be very loose, as for instance 'game', of which Wittgenstein made famous use in *Philosophical Investigations* in demonstrating the impossibility of identifying a single common feature for all uses; while others, such as the taxonomic terms used by botanists and zoologists, may be highly specific. The question arises as to which of these strategies is the more fundamental, and there is, according to Ellen, general agreement that analytic classification is prior to synthetic classification. Continuing with the body-part classification case, it is fairly obvious that synthetic categories such as 'heads', 'fingers', 'teeth', and 'eyes' cannot be formed until such body parts have been initially analytically differentiated out from the body as a whole. On Ellen's account, the application of these body-part-derived synthetic categories to natural phenomena and human artefacts represents an anthropocentric projection onto the world of the human body schema, a move which, though not anthropomorphic in the strict sense, nevertheless suggests something very similar. A set of analytic human body-part categories is subsequently used synthetically to organize the classification of everything else, and, given the ambiguous status of the body discussed earlier, this is surely tantamount to the creation of a universe in the human image in at least some psychological as well as physical sense[5]?

Notwithstanding its plausibility, there is a flaw in this argument for some variety of core anthropomorphism. It arises from a failure on Ellen's part to fully analyse the notion of the primacy of analytic classification. Before elaborating on it, however, we need to clarify exactly what we mean by primacy in this context, since we may be dealing with a purely formal logical primacy, a structural primacy as it were, which our own analysis of the classification problem has disclosed. This would be analogous to geometrical proofs: the squares on the hypotenuses of right angled triangles did not actually only come to equal the sums of the squares on the other two sides after more basic theorems concerning the nature of triangles had been proved; the primacy of these more basic theorems is logical, not temporal. If the primacy is of this order then both kinds of classification may have coexisted from the start. Alternatively we may be dealing with temporal primacy in one of two senses: a) in child development, the level of individual ontogeny, or b) in a cultural historical or evolutionary sense – first humans learned to classify analytically and then later classified synthetically. In interpreting Ellen's argument, only the last of these three alternatives is appropriate; that is to say that the rationale for the whole discussion in anthropology must be that it is actually aimed at unravelling the roots of human classification systems, which can only mean their evolutionary or historical roots. If this is so we are surely on a wild goose chase. Both forms of classification must have coexisted as far back as it is relevant to enquire; the ability to generate synthetic categories must in some sense be ascribed to animals whose behaviours demonstrate the operation of at least such schemata as 'good to eat', 'places to sleep', and 'predator'. In Upper Palaeolithic cave art the earliest figures include both hand-prints and animal species, thereby showing they had both analytic body-part categories and synthetic animal-species categories (Sieveking 1979). It is only in terms of a supposed temporal, diachronic succession of events that a process of anthropomorphic projection based on the priority of analytic classification of body parts can be envisaged: first there were body-part terms, *then* these were turned into synthetic categories, *then* these were applied to the non-human universe. This is in fact what Ellen explicitly claims:

> the very fact that human beings perceive and think anthro-pocentrically in relation to the non-human universe, together with the demonstrable elaboration of human anatomical classification compared to that of other animals, suggests that, generally speaking, the human body is the primary model *in both an evolutionary and logico-operational sense.*
>
> (Ellen 1977:353; my italics)

This scenario cannot be sustained. Use of categories of both kinds and their pre-linguistic precursors as types of discriminatory behaviour have always been necessary for survival. The priority of analytic classification, if it has any, is of a purely logical kind. (The level of individual ontogeny has no bearing on the issue at this point. Whatever the merits of recapitulationist theories of cognitive evolution such as Parker and Gibson's (1979), developmental psychologists do not so far as I know recognize analytic and synthetic stages.) Whether it does have any priority is in fact arguable when we return to what are surely very basic physical sensation classifications. *Hot* (to take a break from *hard*) is not part of anything. It could be argued that the 'whole' in this case is 'consciousness' rather than the body of which *hot* is not a physical part (one might have a classification of all hot parts of the body under a single term, I suppose, but I doubt if it has ever been done) which can be analytically reduced to constituent component sensations, but this would be a highly artificial move. Consciousness has not got bits any more than it is a mirror.

Synthetic classification proceeds in part by identifying phenomena in terms of the physical sensation produced, and every physical sensation which has been classified must yield such a synthetic set. It is, in short, unclear how a notion of a *temporal, evolutionary* primacy of analytically-derived body-part classifications can be coherently sustained; indeed Ellen himself later describes the relationship between analytic and synthetic classifications as 'dialectical' (1977:369).

We must therefore find another interpretation for the data which reveal the widespread use of body-part classifications as general classificatory templates.

USE OF BODY-RELATED CLASSIFICATIONS IN WORLD-LANGUAGE

The first observation to be made is that while body-related categories possess a Janus-faced character, reflecting the body's own dual status as vehicle of consciousness and object of consciousness, when they are in use they must nevertheless be ascribed either WL or PL significance. That is to say, there is no third realm of body-language (BL) in use as such. If it could be shown that all usage of body-related terms in classifying the external world involved their use only in a WL role then the challenge to the physiomorphic account would turn out to be superficial, since this use would not be anthropomorphic in the strict sense. We are, note, not concerned here with behaviour terms, but with body-part, sensory property, and relational terms, although there is admittedly a blurred boundary when it comes to sensory processes such as hearing, seeing, and feeling (see Chapter 3). That use of body-related terms *is* generally restricted in this way to a WL role does in fact appear to be the case in two of the three major contexts in which it occurs – inanimate physical objects and animals. In the third, that of settlement lay-out or architecture, the exceptions to this arise because we are still dealing with the PL realm anyway.

Body part terms are widely used for geographical features: rivers have mouths and headwaters (at opposite ends!), the arms of the sea can embrace a neck of land, mountains have feet, chasms yawn, and rocks have veins of mineral ore. (Sensory property and relational terms need not be considered here, as nobody suggests their use to be anthropomorphic in such contexts.) Such usages are clearly metaphors of a quite orthodox kind based on structural and relational analogies. They carry no PL connotations with them, since they are not 'projections' of human properties onto the physical world in any significant sense. In the case of more complex emotional property terms – angry seas, threatening clouds, peaceful pastures, and sombre hills – the physiomorphic argument is that such psychological categories as *anger, threat, peaceful* and *sombre* are generated in the first place by identification of and with these very phenomena, which simultaneously provide public criteria for labelling the responses they evoke *and* the states of being like them. 'Responses evoked' and 'states of being like' may or may not be identical. Compare *gloomy* with *stormy*: in the latter case the PL term refers to the state, in the former to both response and state. *Glared at* on the other hand refers only to the response, *glaring* being the state. Certainly these terms often involve a notion of agency, but this in itself is not the same as a notion of human-like agency. On the contrary, we are arguing that human-like modes of agency are internalized versions of these in the first place. But here we are shifting prematurely into the behavioural realm. The argument at this point is simply that, as far as basic body classification terms are concerned, their use in classifying geographical and similar natural phenomena is of an orthodox, analogical kind. Nothing psychological, or even organic, follows from mountains having feet – they cannot kick you, stamp on you, follow in your footsteps, or suffer from blisters. The fact that a neck of land is sticking out from an island does not mean that the island is sticking its neck out.

Considering animals (bearing in mind what was said earlier about the *un*self-evident nature of animacy) similar conclusions can be drawn. The use of body-part terms such as head, feet, back, arms, and so on is surely a case of orthodox structural analogising. Where animals possess features lacked by humans (tails, feathers, horns, wings) there is no problem in classifying these parts with non-human body-part terms. Specific animal species may be seen on occasion as paradigm cases of the particular 'modes of being' identified with possession of a certain physical property (slippery eels, slimy toads, cold fish) or their frequent adoption of a certain behavioural reaction (timid deer, sly foxes, and angry wasps). Again, the physiomorphic argument is that whatever the PL meanings of *slippery, slimy,* and *cold* are, they are derived *from* experience of slippery, slimy, and cold phenomena, including these creatures. One can explore slipperiness to some extent by experience of slippery rocks, vegetation, and so on, but to really understand its meaning as a mode of relating to the world one has to go to an excessively and actively slippery animal, to whit – the eel. Insofar as humans are *slippery* in the PL sense, they are so because they have assimilated the nature of the eel, so the ascription of this nature to the eel is hardly anthropomorphic. To say of an animal (a mammal at any rate) that it is 'looking at' something, 'listening to' or 'for' something, or even that it is 'hungry' is hardly anthropomorphic (except for the most unregenerated of behaviourists); to recognise commonalities of state or behaviour between us and other species is not the same as projecting our properties onto them. (That PL connotations may be erroneously carried over along with the WL usage of a term is not denied – to describe a sea anemone as 'grappling' with a prawn may wrongly suggest that the sea anemone possesses active high-level co-ordinational capacities and even motives quite inappropriate for an actinoid zoophyte. Even so this might more correctly be called mammalomorphism than anthro-pomorphism.) In sum, there is no indication that the use of body-related classification for non-human life-forms represents an underlying anthropomorphic process; for the most part it can be accounted for in terms of identification of either structural physical analogies, using the terms in a purely WL sense, or shared states and properties. Ellen may well be correct that body-part classifications provide a basic source of analogies and metaphors for categorizing the natural world: what I am concerned to stress here is that no genuine anthropomorphism is entailed by this.

Many cultures use body-part categories for classifying parts of buildings and as a plan for the layout of villages. Since both of these are in the realm of human cultural artefacts, whatever else this is it is not anthropomorphic projection onto the natural world. The architectural use of body-part terms may often be straightforward analogizing of the sort already noted. There are, after all, formal parallels between the human body and buildings or village settlements: both possess a structural framework (skeleton = beams, posts, rafters, layout of thoroughfares); both have an outer fabric (skin = walls, fences); both have points of entry and exit (mouth, vagina = door, gate); and both have facilities for monitoring the external world (eyes = windows, look-out posts). Functional parallels also exist: both require focal points of functional integration (heart, head = fire-site, market-square, chief's hut, place of religious activity); both involve food management (stomach = kitchen or larder; womb, somewhat more tenuously on food/life equation, = granary), and refuse disposal (anus = waste-tip); while the well/spring = breast analogy is also obvious. These parallels can operate either actively, as a general guide or blueprint for the design and layout of buildings or settlements, or passively, as a basis for classification only. Given the extraordinary variety of human architecture and the range of ways human settlements are designed, there is nevertheless no evidence here of a *common* human body-plan being universally employed to guide and structure their design in either case. At best we have the body used as a sort of mnemonic for the functions and structural features which need to be incorporated. Ellen quotes extensively from Griaule's (1965) study of the Dogon, among whom a village 'should extend north to south like the body of a man lying on his back'; the head is the council house; houses for menstruating women to east and west are the hands; communal altars at the south are the feet; etc. (Ellen 1977:359).

Village layout is a primary instantiation of social structure. Indeed, it is more closely related to this than it is to the human body as such (see Willis 1974)[6]. Social structure may itself be conceptualized in biological terms, but is so varied that the same point applies – there is no common body-part schema operating in all cultures. So far as the present issue is concerned the widespread classification of human settlements and buildings in body terms does not affect the physiomorphism argument, since these are major constituents of the human realm anyway and are constructed to give reality to the meanings and values of particular cultures as much as to meet basic survival needs. Clearly the PL connotations of terms will frequently be retained in these contexts, the village being in some sense an extension of the body, a collective body as it were, with which individuals may identify only somewhat less than they do with their physical bodies. (One is making sweeping generalizations here: this is obviously inapplicable to non-settled cultures, for example. I am to be understood as referring to possibilities, not universal commonalities.) In short, cultural expression of the psychological is not in itself 'anthropomorphic' projection.

The apparent challenge to the physiomorphic model which body-related classification seemed to represent thus turns out to be somewhat superficial, although the simple, initial version of PL as reflexively-applied WL clearly needs modification in the light of the existence of this core set of categories which are from the outset pointing both ways. Here, instead of a transfer from WL into PL we are dealing with the synchronous entry of terms into both vocabularies from a common source which incorporates both realms – the human body. The use of the human body-part classification system in particular as a source of WL categories nevertheless seemed problematical, since it suggested that some kind of 'anthropomorphic' structuring was indeed going on, especially given the body's intermediate status. On further examination this proved illusory. The error lay in the covert assumption that such terms could actually be used in their full ambiguity; in practice such terms are being used either with WL or with PL significance but not with both (indeed the task as we will see later is often to decide which). Secondary connotations from the other realm may sometimes be present, but are not what is being signified. The body itself is in both realms: it does not constitute a realm of its own. Body-language is thus in practice always being used in one realm or other.

SUMMARY

This chapter has been concerned with putting forward the following argument: First, it has been argued that Psychological Language (PL) is problematical on logical and philosophical grounds. Second, a simple account was proposed in which PL is seen as reflexively derivative from World Language (WL). Third, this process was held to be roughly equivalent to Lévi-Strauss's 'physiomorphism' – the assimilation of world properties into 'human nature', the opposite of anthropomorphism. It was seen that such a view had been adumbrated in a wide variety of contexts. This suggested that all PL was ultimately metaphorical in character. But, fourth, in considering basic sensory property terms, this seemed implausible, and it was seen to be necessary to consider the role of the human body itself. Fifth, in the light of this it became clearer that many categories arose simultaneously within PL and WL, acquiring a role in each as a result of the body's own ambiguous status as both signifier and signified. Finally, it was shown that the apparently anthropomorphic use of body-part and body-related categories was illusory since such terms were generally being used either in a WL sense only or, in the case of architectural and village-plan usages, could not count as anthropomorphic since they were being used within the human realm, not imposed on the non-human one. In this final case it was to be expected that some ambiguity between WL and PL usages might persist, the village being indeed the 'body' of the resident community.

As has been noted, physiomorphism as such is not a linguistic process, though it is in the generation of PL that we see it most clearly operating. Later it will be shown how it is language which has facilitated the extraordinary success of physiomorphism as a behavioural amplification strategy. We are now, however, faced with perhaps the most central question of all: if our account of PL is to be fundamentally coherent, it must be possible to account for the emergence of the category 'psychological' itself. It is to this which we turn in the next chapter.

CHAPTER TWO

PERSONS, OBJECTS, AND SIGNALS

Before examining the physiomorphic character of psychological language in more depth, it is necessary to consider further the nature of language itself. While the account which follows has its roots (some of them anyway) in those provided by Wittgenstein, Austin, and other linguistic philosophers, it attempts to apply their insights to psychological issues from a slightly different angle to that adopted in previous efforts of this kind. In particular our concern is with how an utterance is given significance in the context of the relationship between utterer and listener (even in the extreme case of talking to oneself). Although I will be concentrating on spoken language, the same considerations also apply in principle to written language. In recent years there has been a growing appreciation among those psychologists concerned with computer simulation of language (e.g. Winograd 1980) that they had previously been operating with a highly impoverished concept of what language actually was. Somewhat belatedly the implications of Wittgenstein's much quoted dictum 'the meaning is the use' have begun to dawn.[1]

NEGOTIATING MEANING

People simply do not go around saying flatly to one another 'the cube is to the right of the sphere', 'the triangle is above the circle', or similar statements about their visual world now within the capacity of computers to simulate.[2] Human utterances arise within social contexts: people speaking are engaged in living; they are living in a community of speakers similarly engaged and with whom they are attempting to manage psychological relationships of a multitude of kinds; and are doing so in 'real time'. We do not exchange bald propositional statements about our world; we talk in the context of our relationships with other speakers. These other speakers will construe what we say as requiring a response, will ascribe motives to us, and will attempt to endow the utterance with significance in the light of these. The meaning of an utterance is in fact a matter of negotiation between the speaker and the hearer. It might be objected that, surely, the meaning of an utterance is what the speaker intended it to mean and that the hearer either grasps this or not. Not so. Real life conversations not infrequently consist of prolonged negotiations as to the meaning to be given to an utterance by one of the participants. In the course of this process the speaker of the utterance under consideration may change their own initial understanding of its meaning quite radically or they may yield not an inch. In the final analysis however *the* meaning of the utterance, insofar as it can ever be said to acquire one, is that which the community of speakers agrees to give it – and which thereby determines the subsequent transactions between its utterer and that community. Where this process breaks down a speaker may be considered insane, their words being, quite literally, meaningless.

What is meant by saying that meaning is negotiated will become clearer if we consider some examples. A person (A) enters a room and says to someone already in it (B) 'God it's cold in here!' How is B to respond? Here are some possibilities:

  i 'I know – the heater's broken down',
  ii 'I can lend you a sweater if you like',
  iii 'Come here and I'll soon warm you up',
  iv 'Are you joking? It's 80 degrees!',
  v 'I think you are saying I am rejecting you',
  vi 'Stop moaning',
  vii 'You think this is cold – you should have been here last night!',
  viii 'Hey, you're right – I hadn't noticed – switch the heater on',
  ix 'Oh, so you've decided to come home',
  x 'If you'd paid the bill they wouldn't have cut us off!',
  xi 'All the world's cold – it's the human condition'.

Obviously one could go on *ad infinitum.* B's response to A's words can evidently vary from construing it as an implicit request for heat (ii,viii) to overriding them altogether (vi,ix) – in effect refusing to engage in a dialogue on the terms being offered by A. If we leave aside responses of the last kind we are still left with a wide range of possibilities. A can now come back with a response to B's response which can again vary from e.g. 'Yes please' (to ii) to 'Stop trying to butter me up' (to iii). In short, 'God it's cold in here!' might initiate a whole range of dialogues of varying length, emotional quality, and relevance to physical coldness *per se.*

Sticking with this example, let us consider responses iii and v in more depth. In these cases B has (or may be interpreted as having) chosen to construe A's coldness not as physical but psychological in character; A's words are an implicit request for an affectionate cuddle or a statement about his or her attitude to B, rather than a statement about the physical temperature. Let us suppose now that, in case v, A is a patient and B a psychoanalyst. A now rejects response v with some vehemence: 'No I'm not feeling bloody rejected – can't I say anything without you assuming I'm talking about you?' The analytic session continues: B points out how angry A seems to be; A relaxes a bit and begins to concede this. Eventually, by the end of the session, A has come round to agreeing that B's initial response was in fact correct, accepting that his or her opening statement was indeed an expression of a feeling of being rejected. Although this is a very clear case of a speaker's own initial view of the significance of an utterance being renegotiated, in principle I would argue that it applies universally. The fact that much of the time listeners do not choose to challenge speakers in this way (or that speakers win in the negotiation) does not alter the underlying fact that the meaning of an utterance is arrived at by consensus (albeit often unspoken and implicitly understood) between speakers and hearers.

Let us turn to responses i ('I know – the heater's broken down') and iv ('Are you joking? It's 80 degrees!'). In both these cases, though in different ways, B has chosen to construe A's words neither as implicit request for warmth nor as about his or her psychological state, but as indicating a state of affairs requiring diagnosis. B accepts the WL sense of 'cold' but interprets it as a sign of something else. In iv the situation is particularly complex since B disagrees with A as to the existence of genuine physical coldness but remains prepared to concede that A is telling the truth about his or her physical experience. A could reply, 'Are you sure about that?', 'Maybe it is – but I always feel cold these days', or 'I must be sickening for something'. The first of these seems to keep the WL sense in play, the second seems to signal a shift to a PL mode, but the third concedes to B that the 'coldness' being felt is problematic, something requiring diagnosis. Responses vii, x, and xi constitute manoeuvres by B to raise psychological level issues of various kinds using A's words as a starting point; in vii ('You think this is cold – you should have been here last night!') it is as if B is denigrating A's experience or lack of machismo. In x ('If you'd paid the bill they wouldn't have cut us off') A's words are a peg on which B can hang their anger with A and, in xi ('All the world's cold – it's the human condition'), B is switching the terms of the dialogue from the WL to PL level.

MODES OF REFERRING: I

Why spend so much time on this example? The reason is that I believe we can bring some order to this huge variability of interpretational possibilities typical of real life verbal exchanges by identifying three basic modes in which interpretation occurs (though human verbal skills are subtle enough to permit elements of more than one of these to infuse a given response). Two of these are now familiar to us: the World mode and the Psychological mode. The third can be termed the Signal mode. Although when speaking I may intend (or, more accurately, think I intend) my words to be interpreted in one of these modes, my hearers may choose another and respond accordingly. They may do so out of what we commonly call 'misunderstanding', but they may also do so for all sorts of other reasons. This trio is available not only for propositional statements like the one examined above, but for most utterances. 'Get out', for example, could be a simple behavioural instruction, an expression of hostility, or a warning that the ceiling was about to collapse. Since the terms World Language and Psychological Language have already been introduced to refer to the lexical level of language, it is preferable, in order to avoid confusion, to introduce a different set of terms for this broader level of utterance interpretation. The term 'Object mode' (Om) will refer to interpretations which construe utterances as significant in the physical world context, and the term 'Person mode' (Pm) will refer to construal as significant in the psychological world context. The term 'Signal mode' (Sm) requires a little more explanation. It refers to those cases where the subject matter, or referent, of an utterance is interpreted as itself requiring interpretation or diagnosis, that is, is a signal of some sort. In fact, as we will see, in Sm we ascribe 'utterance' status to that state of affairs which forms the subject matter of the utterance itself.

Speakers exercise some control over the mode in which what they say will be interpreted because the vocabularies appropriate to each are not entirely identical, although they overlap considerably, particularly between Object and Person modes, as we have seen in the previous chapter and will be elaborating on further in the next one. Nevertheless, it remains impossible to completely encode *within* an utterance the mode in which it is to be interpreted. Speakers cannot, however hard they try, entirely pre-empt negotiation with their hearers. To attempt to do so would lead to an infinite regress. In a sense these modes constitute 'illocutionary dimensions' within which hearers have to locate utterances *before* they can begin to make sense of them and ascribe them with any significance at all. It is *not* being claimed here that every utterance has three meanings, rather that there are three modes of giving it significance, within each of which the actual meanings given to it may be legion. Real utterances may also be construed in ways which involve more than one referential mode; comments about the weather for instance frequently seem to fuse Pm and Om – the opening line of the song 'Oh what a beautiful morning!' is a general expression of happiness as much as an objective proposition about the climate of Oklahoma. There would be something odd about exclaiming 'what a miserable rainy day!' in a cheerful tone of voice (hence the impact of the line in the film *White Mischief* 'Another bloody perfect day!'). Indeed *some* level of psychological meaning (notably the speaker's mood or cognitive state) is probably implicit in all human utterances – giving rise to the host of illocutionary and perlocutionary terms so lovingly catalogued by Austin (1962). Our perceptions of these are in fact one of the principal factors which determine the referential mode we ascribe to an utterance. But this does not affect my central point; any actual response to 'Oh what a beautiful morning!' will involve choosing one referential mode – 'Gosh, you've cheered up all of a sudden' (Pm), 'Yes – I wonder if it will last' (Om), or 'It looks like our prayers were answered then' (Sm), for example (but see pp. 39-40 for clarification of the status of such examples).

THE MEANINGLESSNESS OF PHILOSOPHICAL EXAMPLES OF MEANING

In a moment I will provide some examples to clarify further what, for brevity's sake, will be referred to as the 'Om', 'Pm', and 'Sm' distinction, but before doing so an important reflexive point has to be made about the status of such examples in writings on the nature of language. In the light of what has just been said about the socially negotiated character of meaning, a question arises as to the nature of the example propositions given in philosophical and linguistic writings – especially writings about the nature of meaning! These become problematical because they have not arisen in the context of 'real life' dialogues between speakers; each exists solely as 'an example utterance in a work on language'. When the work in question is itself about the nature of meaning the difficulty becomes acute. Typically (e.g. Sellars 1980) the writer will provide an example (e.g. 'Socrates is mortal') and proceed to analyse how this acquires its meaning; yet this procedure constitutes a case of *petitio principi*, the fallacy of 'begging the question'. 'Socrates is mortal' only appears to have meaning because there is an unspoken collusion between the writer and the reader regarding that very meaning. 'A is B' would in fact have served as well. Both writer and reader assume in advance some sort of modal meaning (Socrates refers to the Greek philosopher, not a dog or a computer program; mortal is meant in Om etc.). But although it is a grammatically correct sequence of English morphemes, the statement 'Socrates is mortal' inserted out of the blue has no actual meaning; it is not supposed to elicit a response from its reader of the kind 'Physically perhaps, but his thoughts will never die' or 'So – he is not a god after all!'. Any examination of how such an 'example utterance' acquires its meaning thus begs the question by assuming it has a meaning in the first place, an assumption which turns out to be false. My own example, 'God – it's cold in here' is also prone to this criticism; I have assumed that readers will 'fill out' the circumstantial detail (within the constraints of my 'stage directions') and that they will imagine the participants in the proposed dialogues. But of course different readers will vary enormously in how they actually picture these scenes. They could even read it as having a slightly different grammatical structure to the 'normal' one by interpreting the word 'God' as being in the vocative case, i.e., the speaker is addressing God. Perhaps, too, 'cold' is being used in the sense of 'not close to', as in hide-and-seek. My defence is that it is precisely this point which I was striving to illustrate; the example utterance 'God – it's cold in here' requires social contexts to have *any* meaning, and this illustration itself is dependent on a species of social relationship (i.e., a collusion) between you and me in order to be comprehensible. There is a hitherto unspoken agreement between us that you will imaginatively fill out for yourself a fairly orthodox scene in which two characters might be exchanging these words. If you refuse to do so then they too deflate into a mere sequence of English graphemes.

MODES OF REFERRING: II

To return now to Om, Pm, and Sm. I have in the following table tried to provide examples of responses in each mode to an initial utterance. But, in the light of the previous paragraph, it must be stressed that these are responses which, themselves, would 'typically' be construed as being in the mode specified. They cannot be definitively allocated in this way, since they themselves are equally amenable to the same kind of differential interpretation.

At the risk of labouring the point, each of these responses is amenable to the same analysis. Thus to take one example only: 5 (Sm) 'But I had it done last week – something must have caused it', a typical Om response would be 'Well let's have a look and see', a Pm response could be 'It's really worrying you, isn't it?' and Sm 'Yeah, that's very puzzling now you come to mention it'. And so on *ad infinitum*, until the head gasket as such could be lost sight of altogether (or, more fortunately for the initial respondent, simply replaced!).

Obviously many utterances are so explicitly made with a particular intended interpretational mode that responses which

Table 2.1 Examples of responses in each of three referential modes

Utterance	Responses
1. What a lovely sunset!	
	Om: Let me see – mmm it is isn't it?
	Pm: My, you're in a cheerful mood for a change!
	Sm: "Red sky at night, shepherd's delight", my mother always said.
2. Why did he die?	
	Om: Massive brain haemorrhage, sir.
	Pm: There there, you have a good cry about it. Borrow my hankie.
	Sm: Knew a bit too much about Contra drug smuggling is my guess.
3. Do have another drink.	
	Om: I'm not thirsty, thank you.
	Pm: That won't solve anything.
	Sm: So you're not broke after all then?
4. Of course these ideas have been around for a long time.	
	Om: I didn't realise that – can you give me a reference?
	Pm: Stop trying to put me down. Admit just for once that I've come up with something original.
	Sm: Then why have they been so ignored?
5. The head gasket's gone I'm afraid – you'll need a new one.	
	Om: Okay, well fix it as soon as you can.
	Pm: Come off it! Are you trying to con me?
	Sm: But I had it done last week – something must have caused it.

challenge this appear artificial or pathological; nevertheless they cannot be ruled out on logical grounds. There is a phenomenon (which occurs in some psychological disorders and other altered states of consciousness) generally called having 'ideas of reference'. In this the individual may construe all kinds of linguistic (and other) phenomena as Pm or Sm mode references to themselves. Even a sign saying 'No exit' becomes an ominous declaration about the futility of their life, or a piece of conversational small talk like 'the builders are coming next week' becomes a coded message that positive help is at hand – people are talking in parables and allegories; overheard comments become Sm omens (as might physical events); the utterer's own intentions become incidental since they are merely instruments of deeper forces of which they are unaware. It is as if the individual has opted for one mode of interpretation only, or simultaneously opts for two or three.

Other kinds of utterances (notably some of those which Austin called 'performative utterances' such as 'I name this ship the *Mary Rose*' or 'I declare this fête open') do not require spontaneous responses from their audience, being ritual in character. There may be a prescribed verbal response, or perhaps everyone is just expected to applaud. Even so, people may ascribe different kinds of significance to the fact that one person, rather than another, is performing this verbal act. They exchange comments such as 'So – the Chairman of the organising committee got his own way then' and 'Must be down on her luck if she's reduced to this for a bit of publicity'. The manner in which such 'performatives' are executed is, we can see, open to construal in many different ways. Such formal 'performative utterances' are, though, interesting in the present context because they may be seen as attempts, by collective ritualization, to place their meaning beyond negotiation, thereby establishing and/or maintaining a complete consensus. Religious rituals and other ceremonies are the most fully elaborated examples of this kind of language use.

Finally, what of talking to oneself? Here surely no negotiation can occur? But in fact it does, for to talk to oneself is in fact to simulate a dialogue with an analogue 'other'. 'Why am I worried – am I worried? Below the weather that's all – working too hard – stop kidding yourself, something's wrong – why do I think something's wrong? – perhaps I should see the doctor...' (this is admittedly artificial in the sense that talking to oneself, especially if only 'in ones head', is rarely conducted in quite such fully articulated terms, but it nevertheless has this *kind* of format). One is here very obviously negotiating with oneself about the meaning of the phenomenon – in this case whether the 'worry' is Pm or Sm, or even whether the experience warrants the label 'worry' at all. A passage from Gallie (1952), quoting C. S. Peirce, is particularly apposite here:

'All thinking', Peirce writes, 'is dialogic in form. Your self of one instant appeals to your deeper self for his assent'; and again, 'One's thoughts are what he is "saying to himself", that is, is saying to that other self that is just coming into life in the flow of time. When one reasons, it is that critical self that one is trying to persuade; and all thought whatsoever is a sign, and is mostly in the nature of language.' What a man says to himself, he (or his later self) understands: and just as we have

41

to *learn* the meanings of the words which other people
address to us, so we have to learn the meanings of the things
we say, or think, to ourselves.

(1952:82)

What I wish to emphasize in all this is the pervasive presence of
three possible ways of orientating towards the world, of which the
three interpretational modes identified here are an expression –
the Object mode, the Person mode, and the Signal mode. In the
first we are dealing with a world of physical objects and
phenomena, in the second with a psychological world of persons
or 'mental' phenomena, and in the last *with a world of signs and
messages, a world of signals*. The mistake which is almost universally,
if implicitly, made is to assume that these are actually three kinds
of phenomena; that there are three categories of things – objects,
persons, and signals; that there is actually one world of physical
objects, another psychological world of persons and mental
phenomena, and a third world of, in the very broadest sense, signs
or messages. This is reinforced by the fact that the modern
scientific world-view has come to accept that the category 'person'
is only legitimately applicable to fellow members of our own
species and that, though present in crude form in other species,
language is also our exclusive prerogative; hence the third world
becomes equivalent to that of human communication. This is
profoundly mistaken. The fact is that there is only one world, the
phenomena of which, even if private ones, can, in principle, be
interpreted in any of these three modes – however absurd it might
be to do so in particular cases. For much of the Christian era in
Western culture it was quite normal to construe natural
phenomena in Sm as divine allegories, valedictory symbols of
virtues and vices. And of course personhood has been endowed on
a vast range of phenomena from earthquakes to trees, let alone
animals (this choice often being misconstrued as
'anthropomorphism' by modern writers). What we have seen in
the last two centuries is a triumph of Om construal in all except the
circumscribed arena of human behaviour and psychology – and
even there radical Behaviorism made a not entirely ineffective
assault earlier this century. The Middle Ages in Europe,
culminating in sixteenth-century Hermeticism was, by contrast, an
era of Sm dominance, while Pm reigns in 'animistic' cultures.

42

THE ORIGIN OF REFERENTIAL MODES

How has this triad arisen? Language is encountered by its users as a pre-existing phenomenon – although humans invented it, no individual human experienced this invention as such.[3] Its invention was a gradual (if not even-tempoed) affair. Each language user meets an already existing language. It is a world-phenomenon, not a psychological one. *Language itself is thus material for the physiomorphic process.* Language use is comprised of three core components: speaker/listeners (whom I shall refer to as speakers), the utterances themselves, and the referents of those utterances. If there are utterances, then there must be speakers; if there are utterances they must also be about something; and language use implies the capacity of its users to be able to draw these fundamental distinctions. But speakers, utterances, and referents are not classes of objects; they are linguistic roles. Utterances may refer to other utterances, and utterances may refer to speakers etc., and exactly which of all these is going on is precisely what the community of speakers collectively establishes, as argued above. This initiates a very complex situation. Psychological properties are properties of speakers and, as we saw in the previous chapter, speakers acquire and/or identify them by reflexively referring to themselves the properties of the public world *including that of being a speaker.* Being a speaker is thus the necessary condition for knowingly possessing any psychological properties at all. But as all these properties have originated in the public world, then any phenomenon in this world must also possess at least that degree of 'psychologicality' which it has contributed to the speaker's psychology. And since being a speaker and having a psychological existence are now effectively synonymous, it inevitably follows that a degree of 'speakerhood' must be possessed by these public world phenomena also. To simplify the jargon somewhat, 'person' and 'language user' (or 'speaker') are ultimately synonymous. We could not, therefore, have primitively used possession of language as a criterion *for* personhood, since we could never know in principle whether something was really a non-language user or was simply using a language we did not understand. If we have decided, on other grounds, to grant the status of personhood to something, then the onus is on us to *discover* its language and how to communicate with

43

it. But what other grounds can there be? Basically, that it has already served as a source of PL, because in a sense this itself constitutes a communication with us. Its properties *are* its language, and the exploration of these *is*, in part at least, experienced as a learning of its language. (Think of how skilled craftspeople, artists, and performers talk of 'communicating with' their materials and instruments.)

Initially, then, the emergence of syntactic, lexical, language brings in its train a situation where there exists a linguistically construed universe in which all phenomena have continually to be assigned the roles of speaker, utterance, or referent. It is a fluid situation in which only the self-assigned role of speaker/listener is constant, a constancy ensured only insofar as linguistic contact with other speaker/listeners, i.e. the community, can be maintained (though see 'Voices', below). Om, Pm, and Sm have thus arisen directly from the core linguistic roles of referent, speaker, and utterance respectively. To state this in the most general way: the categorical distinctions, seemingly fundamental to all our current thinking, between Mind, Matter, and Message as different ontological levels, are rooted in the requirement that, if we are to be language users at all, the phenomena in our universe must all be assignable – at any given time – to one or other of these core linguistic roles. What has happened since the advent of syntactic, lexical, language (which occured, on current palaeo-anthropological judgement, around 40,000 years ago) has been a constant juggling with these categories.

VOICES

There are a number of issues raised by this which cannot be entered into here, though one in particular should be mentioned: a difficult matter of the phenomenology of language raised by Jaynes (1976). Part of Jaynes's thesis about the origin of modern consciousness involved postulating a phase in the ancient world during which people's behaviour was guided by internal voices. These were construed as voices of gods, and monumental statuary was, he believes, a method for facilitating their production. Jaynes's overall theory has received little subsequent support from either psychologists or anthropologists (though it is widely viewed with affection as a speculative *tour de force*). Nevertheless it does compel us to address what, in our terms, may be stated as the relationship between myself as construed in Pm and in Sm – between my role as a speaker and my role *as an utterance*. This is, on the face of it, an odd question – what does it mean to 'be an utterance'? To 'be an utterance' is to be in a state where the actual role of speaker has been abdicated and the individual has become a messenger, a channel for utterances, not their source. We can find numerous examples of this: Gods, ancestors, the dead, or the 'spirit of the people' being typically given as sources. It is, curiously, easy to forget that language is a matter of *voices*. As Davies (1987) has pointed out, in our culture the written (especially the published) word has in some senses come to prevail over the spoken word since the seventeenth century. In pre-literate societies the voice is absolutely paramount. The language a speaker encounters consists of voices. In the absence of writing the memory of voices carries the culture (along with some artefacts). Although individuals acquire knowledge directly through their own life-experience their knowledge will also include a vast amount of culturally transmitted knowledge encoded in the form of memories of voices. And behind each voice is a speaker.

An individual's own voice is, like the language it speaks, substantially acquired from the culture and from particular individuals within it. Purely physiological factors will affect the timbre and tone range of the voice but within those constraints its apparent uniqueness derives from a blend of genuine innovation and imitation. *My* voice is in some ways difficult to differentiate clearly from others in my repertoire or those of remembered speech acts I have heard. In some respects any speech act, any utterance, involves a choice of voice. In some languages (such as Japanese) this is encoded in a formal way, different modes of address being appropriate to different situations. Even in English this occurs informally: we differentiate between 'respectful' and 'informal' voices, for example, (though we no longer use the 'thou' form of address to indicate the former). This being so it is not surprising that the individual who believes that what they have to say – or what has to be said – is of enormous importance, will select the most prestigious voice in which to say it, (yea verily!). Even further, they may select the most prestigious speaker to determine what to say. The relationships between an individual and the various internalized speakers – people they have loved, feared, admired, etc. – will become quite complex; internal dialogues with them a matter of course. Physiomorphism comes to apply not just to the public world of physical phenomena but to other speakers. Parents, relatives, authority figures, are also internalized, 'identified with', in the same way as animals and sensory properties. If this is so then it is not to be wondered at that in a certain number of cases individuals will, either intermittently or continuously, feel themselves to have become mere agents of one or other of these. And although I am reluctant to pursue it further now (or perhaps ever!), there does seem to be the possibility in all this of some sort of nesting in such a way that access to voices only implicit in a known voice may be gained, and 'ancestral voices' of an otherwise unidentifiable kind be experienced as having 'come through'. However, it must be admitted that a recent account of Christian glossolalia (Samarin 1979) does not support this speculation.

On the other hand contemporary culture is so swamped with voices from the media and the vast numbers of co-inhabitants of urban conurbations, as well as incorporating written alongside spoken language, that the 'self as utterance' is, if not a vanishing experience, one which is construed as pathological, and lacks a clear cultural meaning, (the exceptions being Christian glossolalia and perhaps some forms of singing like jazz 'scat' singing and 'dub').

To summarize the argument: first, the meaning given to an utterance emerges from negotiations between speaker and listener (or listeners); second, although the range of possible responses to an utterance may be very wide, these can be seen to fall into three categories of interpretation which were identified as the Object mode, the Person mode, and the Signal mode; third it was proposed that these originate in a corresponding triad of basic linguistic roles: referent, speaker, and utterance, respectively.

THE ORIGIN OF 'MIND'

The implication of this analysis which is most germane to the understanding of psychological language is that the very existence of the categories 'psychological' and 'physical' is ultimately a necessary corollary of the possession of modern language; it is implicit in the core distinction between the speaker of an utterance and the subject matter, or referent, of that utterance. If speakers are to reflexively refer to themselves *as speakers* a proto-category of 'psychological' (or 'mental') has to be in play *since there is only one actual language available in which all references have to be made.* The first move a being with modern language has to make is the physiomorphic one of incorporating within itself a structure identical with that of language use itself, namely: a speaker, a language, and a realm about which it may speak. Only then does speaking itself have any point. Although 'being a speaker' is only one of such a being's properties, it is on this role that its social identity depends and with which it must primarily come to identify *itself.* In doing so it becomes aware of its personhood. And having done so the phenomena of its experience, whatever else may later be said about them, must *first* be classified within this same scheme, i.e. according to their status as speakers, utterances, or referents of utterances. *This classification task itself then constitutes a central function of actual language use – the collective assessment of the appropriate status to grant the various phenomena which the group, jointly and individually, experience; the creation indeed of a cosmology.* But among these phenomena are their own utterances. Both the psychological co-ordination of the group as a coherent social psychological entity and the successful management of social relationships at the individual level require that there be consensus on the meaning of utterances. Nevertheless, the utterance precedes the establishment of its meaning which, as we have seen, only emerges from negotiation.

An 'ur-category' of 'Mind' must therefore be considered to have originated with the invention of language itself. This required that speakers be able to differentiate between the roles of speaker, utterance, and referent, and identify themselves with the first of these. And for such a speaker to have anything to say they must, at the very minimum, have a technique for identifying their *own* needs and intentions etc., i.e. their own psychological properties. Which brings us full circle back to the physiomorphic nature of PL as discussed in Chapter 1.

It was then by a species of physiomorphic identification with the phenomenon of language itself that the psychological realm of the speaker came to be differentiated from the public physical world. And in its role as mediator between these two, language itself came to constitute the basis of a third world, that of culture. We will consider in Chapter 5 the evolutionary circumstances under which this occured. Possession of language entailed the discrimination of three linguistic roles: speaker/listener, utterance, and referent. The objects of experience (the realm of potential referents) can be assigned any one of these roles, but this assignation cannot be unambiguously encoded in language since it is, as we have seen, a matter for public negotiation. Thus underlying modes of meaning are generated corresponding to this trio of roles which I have called the Person, Signal, and Object modes respectively. The 'psychological' realm, 'Mind', emerges as a realm of experience separate from the physical world as a direct consequence of the necessary requirement that language users identify themselves as speakers. This in turn entails an ability to make reflexive (i.e. self-referential) Person-mode references, an ability directly arising from elementary syntax. *However*, in order to make such references the speaker still has only the language of public phenomena as a resource, as was shown in the previous chapter. The initial physiomorphic move behind the emergence of the category 'Mind' was thus to identify within oneself the property of being a *speaker* (speaking and language being public phenomena).

THE IMPASSE

Discussion of the nature of language is always hampered by the reflexivity of the task. In the present case this is particularly difficult since the task at hand has been to demonstrate the ubiquitous operation of a triad of deep categories of types of modes of referring.[4] Yet this very triad presents itself in different terms according to referential mode. We now arrive at a sort of impasse which I can only attempt to articulate here, rather than resolve. Table 2.2 depicts the possibilities.

Table 2.2 Primary categories

Referential Mode	Categories		
	1	*2*	*3*
Signal	Person	Signal	Object
Person	Mind	Meaning	Phenomenon
Object	Speaker	Utterance	Referent

This triad is seductive and could be seen as corresponding to some traditional metaphysical distinctions: Category 1 being the noumenal world, Category 2 the world of ideas, symbols, and meanings, and Category 3 the phenomenal world of appearances. Drawing such analogies is not, however, the object of the current work and is of doubtful value. The argument here is rather that we have in this triad a basis for understanding how such traditional schemata were generated as a necessary consequence of the emergence of modern human language. This is depicted in Table 2.3.

Table 2.3 Emergence of categories

Protolinguistic roles	Referential modes	Ontological levels
Speaker/listener	Person	Mind
Utterance	Signal	Meaning
Referent	Object	Phenomena

The impasse arises at this point. This sequence (linguistic roles — referential modes — ontological levels) cannot be simply viewed as evolutionary because the first logically entails the second. The protolinguistic roles are primary only in the formal sense that language as such precedes its specific usages. The move from referential modes to ontological levels is more problematic. One might envisage it as being a long-term consequence of living in (and philosophizing about) a linguistically construed universe, a reification or hypostasization of, ultimately, linguistic roles, and in some ways I would want to accept this diagnosis. Our problem is that there is no *transcendental* way of referring to the categories which are present at each point in the succession, and that one cannot conduct any inquiry into one facet of a category (e.g. Person) without that inquiry being construable as concerned with the others (Mind, Speaker). *Psychologically* (i.e. adopting Pm) the categories present themselves as minds, meanings, and objects of experience (phenomena – 'sensations' might be better), semiotically (Sm) as persons, signals, and physical objects (matter), and in Om (i.e. as the basic things in a linguistically construed universe) as language users (speaker/listeners), utterances, and referents of those utterances. But the sequence 'linguistic roles — referential modes — ontological levels' is but a reflexive expression of the same triad: 'objectively' there are linguistic roles, semiotically (in Sm) there are referential modes, and psychologically (in Pm) there are orders of 'being' – ontological levels (i.e. the situation depicted in Table 2.2). The impasse is the impossibility of referring to the triad in a way which is neutral with regard to referential mode. 'Linguistic roles, referential modes, ontological levels' is in itself neither a list of 'things', nor a list of modes of referring, nor a list of ontological levels – it is simultaneously all three. We are not out of the fly-bottle yet.

My aim in this chapter was not, however, to unravel conundrums of quite this profundity, but to see if we can get some purchase on the issue of the origin of the category 'Mind'. This can, I believe, be done by setting the problem in the context of an analysis of the necessary conditions for language use itself, particularly in the central reflexivity requirement that speakers be able to identify themselves as such.

To avoid any misunderstanding it must be stressed that this is not an account of the origin of consciousness or mind, but of the origin of the *category* 'Mind' which facilitates reflexive self-consciousness (Jaynes's (1976) 'analog-I'). While self-consciousness can thus be explained as itself a result of the physiomorphic assimilation of the 'world phenomenon' of 'speakers', this does not mean that prior to this move there were no psychological phenomena; nor does it mean that there was no prior physiomorphic generation of psychological properties; it only means that people were not conscious of these things. Not being conscious that you are conscious is not the same as being unconscious. We will see later that the eventual appearance of lexical and syntactic language was indeed one of the consequences of the prior operation of physiomorphism.

Our original picture of PL being generated by the reflexive application of WL, with a core sensation vocabulary in which neither realm has priority, is thus something of a simplification. It is underlaid by a far more complex system which both generates the PL and WL realms themselves, and maintains an ultimate ambiguity regarding the referential significance of utterances – an ambiguity which it is a constant and central part of our communications with one another to resolve. Bearing that in mind we can, though, now revert to that original picture as providing us with a framework within which to look in more detail at the actual roots of what we, for the most part at any rate, experience as a distinctive PL vocabulary.

CHAPTER THREE

EVERYDAY PSYCHOLOGICAL LANGUAGE

An exhaustive survey of PL would be tedious to write, and the outcome probably unreadable. A more realistic tactic is therefore adopted in this chapter: an examination in some depth of three of the many different sources of PL. This will enable us to appreciate in greater detail both the general character of PL generation and the unique complexity of each of its sources. The three sources selected for scrutiny may be viewed as sampling different levels of a continuum. This continuum extends from a more or less unchanging core of basic psychological concepts up to a level of highly volatile idioms which track current socio-cultural reality. The three selected are: 1) basic motor behaviour, 2) animals, and 3) crafts and technology. As has been noted earlier, single words are only one end of a spectrum of verbal encoding which extends via proverbs and fables eventually to novels and drama – compare 'He's very warm' with 'He's a right Scrooge'. To keep the discussion within manageable proportions we will restrict it largely to single words and short phrases.

The more extended forms do not, I believe, present any new matters of principle, though what does seem to happen is a process of compression over time; Aesop for example took whole fables to encode and communicate particular psychological ideas which eventually came down to us as 'sour grapes' and 'dog in a manger'. While it might be thought at first sight that such expressions are shorthand references to the fables etc. whence they originated, this is not actually so, for they are understood and used by people entirely ignorant of the source. This is not to deny that when the source of such an expression is eventually learned the user may not feel a sense of enlightenment or deeper understanding – this has probably happened to most of us on occasion when discovering where some familiar expression actually came from, but ignorance did not prevent our previous use of it. (Do you know the origin of the expression 'his goose was cooked'?[1] Has that ever stopped you using it?) Famous characters (fictional and real), incidents in myth, drama and history, memorable lines of poetry, and even phrases from political speeches (e.g. Hitler's 'my patience is exhausted') may all enter PL in this way, as encapsulating psychological concepts too complex, initially at any rate, for single words to store. There is no reason to believe, though, that this vast present cultural repertoire of PL constitutes anything other than a superstructure built upon the basic physiomorphic process described in Chapter 1.

BASIC MOTOR BEHAVIOUR

It will be sufficient to examine two examples: visual behaviour and basic motor schemata. The first, visual behaviour, may be felt barely to count as a 'motor behaviour' at all, but is a highly appropriate starting point since it constitutes the source for much of the very core of the PL we use to refer to knowledge (and ignorance); we are enlightened, light is shed, wise words are illuminating, or we are completely in the dark, blind to the obvious. The equation of light to knowledge is of course rooted in the simple fact that knowledge of our physical surroundings is primarily visually mediated and this requires the presence of light – intimately related to sunrise, as the notion of truth 'dawning' indicates. As previously explained, we should be particularly wary of ascribing temporal primacy to the WL senses of terms in our basic sensation language. This is especially true of what we might term 'Light-Language'; at the outset of human knowledge acquisition, 'to know' and 'to see' were surely virtually indistinguishable. In the phrase 'I see', the distance between the referential modes is minimal.

The Oxford English Dictionary lists fourteen primary meanings for 'see', of which 10 are PL; for 'look' half the meanings, i.e. 4 out of 8, are PL. Tables 3.1 and 3.2 list the majority of PL uses of perception terms, including, in addition to expressions involving perceptual verbs (*see, look, watch, view* etc.) adjectives referring primarily, in their WL senses, to qualities of light.

Table 3.1 Perception-based PL: OED PL senses of SEE

Sense	Example
1. Learn	'I see they've discovered a new cure for flu'
2. Discern mentally	'Do you see what I mean?', I can't see any point in it', 'Now do you see why he did it?'
3. Experience	'I'll never see thirty again', 'I never thought I'd see the day when a thing like that could happen'
4. Grant interview etc.	'I'll see him tomorrow', 'I must see my solicitor'
5. Imagine	'I can just see myself in ten years' time'
6. 'Recognize as tolerable'	'do not see being made use of'
7. Escort	'Let me see you home'
8. Make provision for	'I will see that it is done', 'See that my things are ready'
9. Make examination of	'must see into it', 'I'll see what's going on'
10. Reflect	'Let me see now', 'I will see about it' (as prevarication)

Although 6. is not perhaps entirely clear, one is as usual impressed with the perspicacity of the OED's compilers in teasing these out. Nevertheless the imposition of a definitive ten meanings is a little artificial, as these meanings tend to glide into one another rather imperceptibly (a point to which we return below). Common expressions using *see* in a PL sense also include the following: *to see — a way out, the point, what you're driving at, red, clearly, through, dimly, eye-to-eye, to oversee;* (and note also: *far-sighted, short-sighted,* and *lose sight of*).

From the accompanying tables it is fairly clear that this section of the PL vocabulary is primarily concerned with elucidating the following psychological topics: a) quality of knowledge as such, b) quality of individual consciousness in relation to particular objects of knowledge, c) quality of personality particularly with respect to degree of intelligence and/or general competence at managing a task or social situation (i.e. centring on the individual as a knower), d) interpersonal attitudes (particularly in the various ways of referring to interpersonal 'looking'). Underlying all this is a clear equation of light to consciousness itself.

This suggests that a primary move in the physiomorphic process was a physiomorphic incorporation of light, and the sheer directness of the relationship between being conscious and having visual experience highlights once again the inadequacy of a crude

Table 3.2 Other visual-based PL

___

1. PL senses of 'light'
   in the l. of, shed/cast/put etc. a fresh/new/different etc. l., enlighten, to highlight
2. PL senses of 'look'
   to look — at, askance at, down at/on, into, out for, up to, daggers at, forward to
   to look at — in the wrong way, it back-to-front, from a different angle, in the best/worst possible light, from another (etc.) point of view, like this
   a dirty look, outlook (*as in 'his* outlook *on life is very pessimistic'*)
3. PL senses of 'view'
   to view, views (=*opinions*), point of v., dim v., long/short-term v., review, narrow v., broad v., distorted v., rosy v.
4. PL senses of 'watch'
   to watch out for, to w. what you're saying
5. PL senses of other vision-related verbs
   to observe, to focus/to get in focus, to frown on, to get things in perspective, to glimpse, to picture to oneself, to be blind to, to be blinded by (*e.g. science*), to wink at, to be in the dark, to envision, to visualize, to imagine
6. PL adjectives referring to quality of light etc.
   bright (=*intelligent*), brilliant, dazzling, dim, enlightened/ enlightening, glaring, gloomy, illuminating, shining, sparkling, staring one in the face, (*some of these, such, as* dazzling, *can of course be 'verbed' into* to dazzle)
7. PL terms referring to eyes
   wide-eyed, open-eyed, misty-eyed, turn a blind eye to (*recent, fr. Nelson*), blind-spot, cross-eyed (=*tired and confused from prolonged concentration*) green-eyed (=*jealous*), tip the wink
   (*Properly belonging in the next section of the chapter are*: cod-eyed, doe-eyed, hawk-eyed, snake-eyed)
8. Other visual PL
   seer (=*prophet*), to appear (*e.g. 'it* appears *to me that...')*/apparent, mirage (*e.g. 'he realized that her love for him was but a* mirage'), tunnel vision (*modern*), discerning, inner eye, visionary

___

Note: No claims are made for the completeness of this table.

'metaphorical transfer' account. Experience of dreams and visual imagery even in the absence of an external light source would surely have seemed to entail a quite literal incorporation of light. Furthermore, the quality of one's consciousness would then have seemed to be a function of the amount of light thus incorporated – for it would be this which determined how much one could 'visualize', i.e. the range of one's knowledge and understanding. Such a notion becomes quite explicit in oriental religious philosophy; in *The Secret of the Golden Flower* (Wilhelm, trans. 1984) the key to enlightenment is quite directly portrayed as being the cultivation of meditation techniques which maximize the internalization and inner circulation of light, with no distinction being made between PL and WL senses of the term. The word *wise* is also, we can note here, apparently derived from an Indo-European root meaning 'to see' (see Appendix A). In both Eastern and Western religious symbolism haloes and auras surround the heads or bodies of the holy. This is more than a mere artistic device for scriptures, and hagiographies make it quite explicit that such phenomena were genuinely believed to occur, even if the radiances in question were visible only to observers who had themselves achieved a high spiritual status. (It is possible that this belief arose as an over-literal understanding of a prior artistic convention, though this seems, prima facie, unlikely. Even so it would not matter seriously if this were the case, since the choice of this convention and the readiness with which it was interpreted in such a way still testify to the intrinsic power of the light= consciousness equation.) The eyes, as light-receptors, are also popularly conceived as light-transmitters – and certainly as transmitters or indicators of their owner's state of consciousness.

At heart, we are dealing here with a most fundamental psychological construct: the distinction between consciousness and unconsciousness; and this was – and perhaps could only have been – initially articulated in terms of the light-darkness polarity, the diurnal waking-and-sleeping cycle cementing the connection inseverably. There is an ambiguity in the status ascribed to light in the Genesis creation myth: it may be considered to be the ontological *prima materia* – the ground of physical existence – but it may also, and perhaps more sophisticatedly, be taken as the epistemological *prima materia* – the ground for all consciousness of what exists. But one does not have to be a very subtle philosopher to recognize that this ambiguity dissipates if, as Berkeley held, '*esse* is *percipi*' (1710; 1962 edn:66) – if 'to be is to be perceived'.

It may at this juncture be objected that blind people are as conscious as the rest of us, thereby demonstrating that conscious- ness is not actually dependent on physical light. With this I would immediately concur. As Helen Keller proved, a sense of touch alone is sufficient. Our concern is with the nature of the PL in terms of which consciousness is construed, not directly with consciousness itself. Curiously the cultural construal of blindness has often involved endowing the blind, because of their evident possession of consciousness, with enhanced inner vision as prophets and seers. We must not forget that the blind exist in a sighted community and it is this which generates PL. In a 'country of the blind' – supposing it to be viable – PL would develop in a quite different way: their God would perhaps begin not by announcing 'Let there be Light', but by making a noise. The noise-based PL, which I am not discussing here, would presumably be more elaborated, and the sound–silence polarity be as central as the light–dark one is now.

What I have been suggesting is that the phenomena of light, its absence, and its varying qualities, constitute a central, perhaps *the* central, raw material from which we have physiomorphically constructed our 'psychology'. They come to occupy this central role by virtue of the extraordinarily direct phenomenological relationship between light and consciousness itself. Once established as a core PL construct, the ancillary perceptual behaviour vocabulary of looking, watching, and seeing etc. falls into place almost automatically as a mode of referring to qualities of knowledge and its acquisition, as well as of interpersonal attitude and relationship. The vocabulary of light-quality similarly constitutes a vocabulary of personality and performance descriptors. Regarding the issue of WL primacy, while relatively recent additions to this section of the PL vocabulary such as 'turning a blind eye' (from Nelson's behaviour at Trafalgar) and 'tunnel vision' (from research on perception) clearly arose from a straightforward 'metaphorical transfer', the initial equation of light to consciousness and many of the basic PL uses of *see* and *look* are harder to account for in this way. The distinct PL and WL meanings more likely separated out from an initial all-embracing usage, in which choice of referential mode alone determined their significance (see Chapter 2). In other words, one must strongly doubt if 'Can you shed more light on this point?' could ever have meant only 'Can you hold the candle closer to the needle?', or 'Look at it another way' meant only 'Hold your head in a different position'.

One of the major areas in which motor-behaviour has generated PL is manual behaviour. This is no doubt a commonplace observation in the wake of Piaget, since the centrality of sensori-motor schemata in the aetiology of the first genuinely psychological ones is not something which even his most ardent critics (such as Brainerd 1978) would take issue with in any fundamental way. It is nevertheless worth reminding ourselves of quite how much of our PL language originates from this source (often pertaining to basic cognitive phenomena and operations):

> *to feel, to grasp, to lose one's grip, to handle, to pick up, to let drop, to point out* (and *to indicate*), *to hold, to manage* (= *handle*), *to maintain* (= *hold in the hand*), *to manipulate, to keep a tight/firm grip, to juggle, to knock, to rap, to hit, to move* (though this is rather more general, as perhaps is *to feel*), *to take a swipe at, to throw, to catch, to put one's finger on, to scratch the surface, to poke about, to fumble, to tie up, to put, to put down, to place, to unravel, to cling to, to seize, to press (the point home)*, plus *to apprehend* and *to comprehend* (from Latin praehendere = capable of grasping). *To elbow one's way in* and *to cold shoulder* possibly belong here too!

From the other extremity we get:

> *to kick, to stand (one's ground/up to/for/take a), to understand, to stumble, to walk over, to jump (on/over/to conclusions), to take the next step* (also, of course, *'a step in the argument', 'a step in the dark', 'a step in the right direction'* etc.), *to tiptoe* (e.g. 'we will *tiptoe* lightly over this problem'), *to dig one's heels in, to run (over/through/ up against/ out of ideas/ back to the beginning/ ahead of oneself* etc.), *to stamp on/out, to put the boot in, to leap, to trample, hopping mad, to skip, to side-step, to put one's best foot forward, to tackle, to lose ones footing, to trip up, footloose, footling, weak-kneed, assiduous* (cognate with Latin *sedere* = to sit).

The related area of locomotion in general provides:

> *to follow, to lose/keep/be on the — track of, to wander, to keep pace with, to keep up with, to come across, to catch up with, to explore, to*

stagger, to lead, to lead astray, to side-track, creepy, to fall, to come on apace.

There is also a rather miscellaneous group of concepts such as:

to find, to lose, to keep, to stay, to side with.

Freudians have long pointed out the presence in everyday language of oral 'metaphors' such as:

to swallow/hard to swallow, to chew over, gullible (related to *gullet*), *to stick in one's gullet* (or *craw*), *to stomach, hard bitten,* and *sucker* (these tend to support Erikson's view of the oral stage as being to do with trust/mistrust, particularly the equation of believability to ease of swallowing, and to be *tight-lipped* is to be adopting a resistant sceptical attitude). In addition there are the personality descriptors *sweet, sour,* and *bitter* (which lead on to culinary language, an area dealt with later).

For completeness sake I suppose one should also mention: *hard-nosed, to stink, to smell to high heaven, to sneeze at, to get up one's nose, to poke one's nose in, to nose around, to sniff out, to get a whiff of, snooty,* and *snotty-nosed.* Defecatory functions are not surprisingly a source of negative PL terms: *pissed off, crappy, shitty* (and the person-descriptors of someone as a *shit* or an *arse-hole*), although they are not very numerous (but see Bornemann 1976 on the use of defecatory imagery in referring to money – and vice-versa).

The majority of basic motor schemata terms in PL are in that category of concepts discussed in Chapter 1, in which the body operates as an intermediary between the two realms. As behaviour they are public phenomena, but as behavers we cannot differentiate between their overt and 'private' meanings – they are a psycho-physical unity. It is not uncommon, though, for such terms to possess more than a simple binary character as PL and WL concepts; their PL meanings can occur at several levels, the more abstractly psychological of which represent a deeper assimilation. This is evident for example in the perception-based language. Consider the following hypothetical contexts for the term 'see':

a) Two people are trying to find a way across a river; one says 'I can't see how we're going to do it'. 'See' here is almost literal – the speaker cannot physically 'see' a route across.

b) Two people are looking at a map; one says 'Ah! I see where we are', and points to a spot on the map. This is slightly less of a literal 'seeing'; it is a sort of decoding. Nevertheless, the point of reference is an external object, the map, and overt visual behaviour is still involved.

c) Two people are looking at timetables; one says 'Ah! I see how you can do it!', and proceeds to explain how a journey can be undertaken. This is a further stage removed from literal 'seeing' – the 'seeing' is the result of complex cognitive operations on a variety of information. The timetables are, though, still an external point of reference for both parties.

d) Two people are discussing their relationship; one says 'I don't see how we can go on living together the way we are'. At this point we feel the physical seeing sense has almost been abandoned altogether. We are dealing with purely internal envisioning; the information on which the statement is based is perhaps known to both parties but is not in the form of immediate visible phenomena.

e) Two people are having an argument about politics; one says 'I cannot see how you can possibly believe that!' This strikes me as even further from the physical seeing sense than the previous case; in d) we might imagine the speaker trying to form a mental picture of an acceptable future in some sense, but here even this vestigially literal visual meaning has gone. This is 'seeing' in a quite abstract 'psychological' sense, translatable with little loss into 'understand' – a term derived from quite a different behavioural arena, but which is now similarly distant from its source.

'Seeing' has become a term to refer to some very basic type of mental act, but one to which it is impossible to refer more 'literally', since all potential synonyms or attempted characterizations will be couched (like 'understand', or the OED's 'discern' – from a Latin root meaning 'sift') in terms likewise derived from behavioural – or other WL – sources.

Such terms as *see, hold, look,* and *follow* slither from one end to the other of a continuum between literal physical and abstract psychological meanings. By the time we are self-conscious enough about the issue to begin examining them, they have become irremovably ensconced in key positions in the very repertoire of operations in which our examinations are conducted. We are then

60

faced with absurd reflexivities – trying to see what 'see' means, trying to hold onto the meaning of 'hold', looking for the meaning of 'look', following the meaning of 'follow' round in circles. (Ryle (1949), on the contrary, held that 'literal' and 'metaphorical' psychological usages of 'see' are self-evidently distinct.)

ANIMALS

The intimacy of our psychological involvement with animals is difficult to overestimate; they are, as Lévi-Strauss allegedly said, 'good to think'. It is an involvement which operates at many levels: we eat them; we use their body parts as a source of material for clothing, tools, decoration, and even scent (musk); we use them as means of transport and general energy resource; they entertain us; and they keep us company. But, as we saw in Chapter 1, they also serve as behavioural models and as embodiments of existential states: we use them as teachers. Their primary contribution to PL has thus been twofold: a) via behaviour, particularly locomotion, terms, and b) as a template for personality typologies.

As far as the first of these is concerned the physiomorphic process begins with behavioural emulation and the generation of an extensive vocabulary referring to the characteristic behaviours of different species. Lonsdale (1981) has provided us with an extensive review of, to use the title of his book, *Animals and the Origins of Dance.* In traditional cultures dances are a, perhaps *the*, central procedure by which group identity and culture are maintained. Every major life event, from birth via puberty, courting, and marriage, to death is marked by dances, as too are hunting, war-making and other activities (including the marking of seasons). In all these dances animals are central (my favourite title is an Arnhem Land aboriginal dance called 'crab in a hole'). They codify and explore the cultural meaning and significance of different species and different animal behaviours. Masks, body-paint, dress, and noises, as well as the dance-steps themselves, represent and incorporate animal behaviour and form, often in the most literal manner (e.g. dressing in its skin). Dancing is *the* communal activity *par excellence*. In modern industrial cultures this has largely atrophied. Only ballroom dance fans still do the foxtrot. This is not to claim that nobody dances any more of course, but that its role has become peripheral. It is either professionally institutionalized or a purely hedonistic activity engaged in at parties, (although ritual military parades like Trooping the Colour ought also, technically, to be considered a form of dancing).

From the viewpoint adopted in this book the traditional notion of possession by animal spirits, often an integral part of dance, comes into focus as the phenomenological face of conscious physiomorphic assimilation. To know an animal, become it. The notion of physiomorphism can, I suggest, integrate a whole range of behaviours from dance, through styles of dress and ornamentation, to yoga postures (asanas). In every case individuals are directly assimilating to themselves the properties and characteristics of external world phenomena, and paramount among these are animals. Some cultures have become virtually symbiotic with a specific species, like the Nuer with their cattle, Genghis Khan's Mongols with their horses, and other nomadic people with sheep, goats, or camels. The earliest forms of cosmological thinking were, as far as we can tell, in terms of what Campbell (1984) called the 'animal powers'. From the Upper Palaeolithic cave art of the Dordogne and northern Spain to the native Australian's 'dream-time', from Amazonian Xingu myths (O. and C. Villas Boas 1974) to the animal-headed gods of ancient Egypt and Hinduism, animals dominate religious thought. The traditional way of viewing this has been to see it in terms of 'anthropomorphism'. Our argument has been the reverse, that the anthropomorphism in it is the result of recursive and reflexive cultural elaboration of what is essentially a physiomorphic process. (Jung used the term 'theriomorphism' to mean something similar, the possession of an animal 'soul', but this is inadequate for our purposes as it is too restrictive and in invoking the concept 'soul' rather begs the question of how *that* originated.) The psychological meaning of a species becomes progressively more distanced from the physical animal itself – much as the meaning of 'see' becomes distanced from physical seeing. Thus the core Christian symbolism of Christ as the Lamb of God, that image of a lamb with a cross over its shoulder which adorns all Anglican altars, bears little obvious relationship to real lambs, and as time proceeds the image requires more and more elaborate exegesis to retain any meaning. But the 'Lamb of God' image, like the foxtrot but unlike 'seeing', is now severed from its source, at least in urban industrial cultures. We will be returning to these topics in Chapter 5.

I do not, however, wish to repeat here the arguments put forward in Chapter 1. The PL legacy of our involvement with animals must be understood as only a partial reflection of their actual psychological importance to us, and indeed, as this has apparently declined in our culture over the last two centuries, the live PL vocabulary itself has probably begun to shift correspondingly ('hold your horses!' has a definitely dated ring to it now). It should be noted that folk-etymology is often unreliable as far as actual word origins are concerned, but in this realm the very fact that a false folk-etymology has taken root might be taken as evidence of the psychological, if not the historical, connotations of a word. I have though tried to avoid these; *to carp* has nothing to do with the fish, and the etymology of *fly* dissolves into a complex of words to do with fleeing and flying. All the same, many species names have been 'verbed' and become part of PL:

> *to ape, to badger, to beetle, to beaver, to chicken out, to crane, to crow, to dog, to duck, to ferret, to fox, to hare, to hog, to horse about, to hound, to lionize, to louse up, to monkey around, to ram, to rat, to rabbit, to rook, to weasel, to worm,* plus, to some extent (according to the OED), *to cow* (but not coward); *to quail,* however, is of unknown origin, while *to snipe* refers to the shooting of snipe rather than the behaviour of snipe themselves.

Animal locomotor behaviour gives us:

> *to burrow, to creep, to dive, to flutter, to fly, to gallop, to hover, to pounce, to scamper, to scuttle, to skulk, to slither, to strut, to swoop, to trot, to wriggle,*

while animal noise-terms are typically used to characterize human speech style:

> *to bark, to bleat, to bray, to coo, to crow, to drone, to grunt, to hiss, to mewl, to neigh, to purr, to roar, to squawk, to twitter, to warble, to whinny.*

A few other verbs which refer to behavioural idiosyncrasies of specific animals, such as styles of eating or grooming, could be added, such as *to gobble* (turkeys), *to chew the cud* (cows), *to nestle* (birds), *to preen* (poultry birds in particular), and *to bury one's head in the sand* (ostrich). The last of course is based on a complete misunderstanding of ostrich behaviour, but, as a behaviour which is definitely not recommended, the emphasis is on not doing it, not on adopting it!

Although these are all PL terms, or can at least carry psychological connotations, they are not all of the same status. In some cases from the first group the PL usage results from the species name becoming first used for a fairly specific category of overt behaviour and only then becoming PL (*to duck, to ram*), with others a more general species style of behaving is encoded (*to badger, to hound*). The use of animal noise-terms for speech qualities is especially significant for our thesis as it implies a lurking animal identity behind the human speaker, the ascription of a particular animal-style or orientation to the listener. Most of these noise-terms are negative in their connotations (though not all – *to coo* and *to purr* may be positive and *to roar* can be both positive and negative), implying that the person speaking in this way has partially lapsed from human status.

Adjectivally we can describe people as:

bird-brained, hare-brained, catty, cocky, cuckoo, crabbed, fly, foxy, horsy, lousy, mousy, mulish, piggish, ratty, sheepish, shrewd, shrewish, sluggish, tigerish, a toady, waspish, (but not *ravenous*), plus proverbial comparisons: *happy as a lark, strong as an ox, slippery as an eel, timid as a deer, free as a bird, cold fish, eagle-* or *hawk-eyed, doe-eyed, busy as a bee, lynx-eyed, lion-hearted, vain as a peacock.*

This last category brings us close to the use of animals as a template for classifying personality traits and types. There are of course a number of such uses which are primarily abusive (*ass, bitch, dog, hog, louse, pig, rat, shark, skunk, worm*) or lightly derisory (*monkey, shrimp*), but both Western and Oriental astrology have drawn heavily, even primarily, on animals to provide sophisticated personality typologies. Occasionally of course a term like *mole* can acquire a quite specific popular meaning. In the West, eight of the twelve zodiacal signs are animal based (Aries, Taurus, Cancer, Leo, Scorpio, Sagittarius (depicted as a centaur archer), Capricorn, and Pisces), while the Chinese system, based on a twelve-yearly rather than twelve-monthly cycle, is exclusively zoological, the sequence being: snake, horse, sheep, monkey, cock, dog, boar, rat, ox, tiger, rabbit and dragon (this last being, admittedly, mythical – the origins of Chinese dragons must alas be passed over here, but there is a connection with lightning). Days and hours are similarly linked to different fauna, including many not in the yearly cycle such as bat, wolf, and worm. This enables one to be characterized as e.g. (in the author's case) someone born in the hour of the rabbit on the day of the cock during the summer solstice season (seasons not being labelled in animal terms) of the year of the metal snake. The connection between animals and personality can be mediated via the individual's physiognomic appearance, as in G. B. della Porta's *De Humana Physiognomia* (Porta 1586) with its illustrations of the ox-man, the dog-man, and the sheep-man, etc. (a rhinoceros-man appears in one of the later editions). (Sheldon's *Atlas of Man* (1954) contains distant echoes of this in his identification of particular somatotypes by names such as 'Palaeolithic Tiger' and 'Dugongs and Manatees'.) By this stage in the development of PL the relative weights of physiomorphism and anthropomorphism become, not surprisingly, difficult to disentangle. For individuals bearing morphological similarities to particular species (the massively built 'ox', the slim wiry 'snake', or the lithe and long-legged 'deer'), the species itself may well have originally provided a model, or at least an inspiration, as how best to exploit this physique. The problem is though deeper than this: how was anybody to behave at all? Lacking a species-specific behavioural repertoire our early ancestors simply had to construct one out of environmental phenomena, and, among these, animals were the most important (see Chapter 5).

To avoid misunderstanding by anthropologists I must stress that I am in no way disputing that contemporary animal classification systems and the symbolic significance particular cultures may attribute to certain species such as pangolins and cassowaries are intimately bound up with, and expressive of, social structure (see Willis 1974 for an accessible analysis of this). Nor am I denying that the behaviour and character of animals as portrayed in myths and folk-tales is frequently 'inaccurate' and 'anthropomorphic' in our terms. What I am asserting is that animals played a very central part in the construction of human self-consciousness, providing a massive natural library of possible behaviours, properties, and states. The animal realm was, furthermore, perceived as a community, not a mere conglomeration, of beings. It provided models for social as well as individual behaviour and, via that, social structure itself. (I suspect that in a sense I may be arriving at Lévi-Straussian positions by the back door here.) The notion of the animal realm as a community is nowhere more apparent than in relation to birds. The community of birds is seen world-wide as comprising a community of personality types – in our culture consisting of thieving magpies, wise owls, noble soaring eagles, deadly efficient hawks, beautifully singing larks and nightingales, gentle doves, squabbling and quarrelsome starlings, vain peacocks, combative robins, silly, but obstinate, geese, and even more stupid chickens, to name but the more obvious. (Chaucer's *Parlement of Briddes or the Assembly of Foules* (rep. 1893) and the Sufi mystic Attar's *Conference of Birds* (1985) constitute higher cultural expressions of this theme.) Birds represented a problem for physiomorphism since their most obvious feature, that they could fly, was the one behaviour that could not be physically emulated. Perhaps for this very reason they became symbols of that part of us which was not, it seemed, earthbound: a psyche, or soul, or spirit (e.g. the dove in Christianity, and the various bird-hieroglyphics used to represent the soul in ancient Egypt)[2]. My central argument is that the elaborate cosmological systems which ultimately evolved to maintain, explain, and explore the 'human' – at both the social structure level and the individual psychological level – were constructed out of the 'natural' world, not, in the first place, imposed or projected on it 'anthropomorphically'. There was simply no 'anthropos' to do the 'projecting'; it had to discover itself in the natural world (including its bird-soul) before it could begin to juggle with, rearrange, reassign, and reevaluate the meanings of what it found there.

CRAFTS AND TECHNOLOGY

While the basic behavioural vocabulary and familiar natural phenomena provided a relatively stable core to PL, it is continually being augmented by new terms derived from areas of novel communal experience, among which the technological and scientific have been particularly powerful in recent centuries. Somewhat intermediate in status are terms derived from long-established crafts, trades, and domestic activities like cooking. The rate of PL change is presumably closely related to broader social change. Although PL terms may eventually become obsolete following the disappearance of their sources there is considerable inertia and in modern times at least the PL has expanded, terms drawn from obsolete or long-vanished sources persisting (e.g. the hunting expression *to pass the buck*). In the case of *to have someone taped* the current popular understanding is probably 'to have someone's words on record so they can't wriggle out and change their position', not 'to have someone tied up', as it did originally – in this case the metaphor has shifted but the PL meaning has remained almost, but not quite, constant. The kind of PL to be considered here is far more clearly of an orthodox metaphorical character than either of the previous sources. A full review of all terms of this type is again impossible, but two traditional crafts are of particular interest: fire-control and cooking/food processing.

a) Fire-control

Fire-control terms have proved especially useful for the encoding of what we now term arousal states, and constitute an extension of the temperature-based PL (*hot, cold, tepid, frigid, lukewarm, icy*). They include the following:

> *to blaze up, to burn, to be burnt up/out/into one's memory, to burn one's fingers, to dampen down, to douse, dying embers* (e.g. 'her smile rekindled the *dying embers* of his passion'), *fiery, flaming, to fan the flames, to flare up, to fuel, to ignite* (e.g. 'his words *ignited* the passions of the crowd'), *inflammatory, to kindle, to light* (e.g 'I just want *to light a flame* in your heart'), *to rake over the ashes, red hot, to rekindle, scorched, searing,* (e.g. especially in the phrase *heart-searing), singed, to smoulder/ smouldering, to spark off, to stoke up.*

The psychological importance of fire is extraordinarily far-reaching; it has become a symbol of both life and destruction. For half a million years – perhaps twice as long – our ancestors have been meditating on the enigmatic character of fire, making of it an image of both Hell and purification. The elder Pliny waxed eloquent on it, ending 'O fire, thou measureless and implacable portion of nature, shall we rightly call thee destroyer or creator?' (quoted in Farrington 1961)[3], while the palaeoarchaeologist Alexander Marshack has more recently written:

> fire is "alive." It must be tended; it needs a home and place out of the great winds, the heavy rains, the deep snows; it must be constantly fed; it sleeps in embers and can die, yet it can also be blown back to life by the breath; it can burn a hand; it sputters angrily and brightly with animal fat; it dies entirely in water; it whispers, hisses or crackles, and therefore has a variable "voice"....To a man with fire, then, there is a continuous involvement in a complex, dynamic process which creates its varying, yet "artificial," demands, relations, comparisons, recognitions, and images.
>
> (Marshack 1972: 112–3)

Fire shares the role of primary image of 'the life-force' with the wind, and Hewes (1973) notes that breath-control is closely involved in fire-control (the wind/breath relationship being very close of course).

b. Cooking and food

The ways in which the cook treats food serve as one way of schematizing the ways we can treat people, while if oral behaviour is as fundamental as psychodynamic theorists believe it is not surprising that food qualities serve as a template for psychological ones. We can grill people, let them stew in their own juice, watch them simmering with resentment, or land them in a pretty pickle. Other terms from this source include:

> to baste, biting off more than one can chew, brewing, taking the biscuit/cake, to carve up, close to the bone, to cook up, to cream off, crusty, curdling (as in blood-curdling), dish out/up, to fork out, fruity, gone off (or a bit off=bad, dubious), half-baked, ham-fisted, hard-boiled, hard cheese, on ice, juicy, to ladle out, meaty, milksop, mincing one's words, near the knuckle, nutty as a fruit-cake, peppery,

the proof of the pudding, to roast, salty, saucy, scald, seethe, spicy, spoon-fed, stale, to stir, sugary, a tough nut to crack, treacly, tripe, vinegary.

The humble egg deserves special attention. Egg-phenomena include being laid, incubating, hatching and cracking (all PL terms). It is the fact that the egg's contents cannot be seen which is central to its fascination – some hidden process is going on which cannot come to light until a fixed time has elapsed (oven itself comes from ova=egg after all). It occurs widely as a symbol in creation myths, alchemy, and psychotic delusions, facilitated partly by the further equation sun=yolk. One crucial comparison is with the head (hence 'addle-pated', 'a bit cracked', and 'egg-head'), the skull/egg parallel providing a way of conceptualizing an internal location of activity with no external manifestations, an image of secrecy – behind impassive masks exist the plans and schemes which the person is incubating, plots they have laid, which will eventually hatch. Nuts and shellfish share this, and, along with eggs, are the archetypal safes, containers of hidden value, to be cracked. But of the exhausted, worn out, ruined individual we say they are an empty shell, or a husk. Beck (1978) cites an example of the incorporation of the egg=head analogy into ritual in New Guinea:

the egg-to-bird progression is linked by analogy to ancestral human grave/shrines. The skull of a deceased kinsman is seen to resemble an egg buried in a dark place. The spirit of the dead person is then seen to be released from this "shell" to "fly" upward as a hatched bird flies after leaving its shell.

(1978:88)

In addition to fire and cooking, weaving warrants a passing mention since it was for a long time the most complex household activity routinely engaged in, and served as a source for labelling cognitive processes. The following two contrived sentences combine most of the weaving and textile terms currently in use: 'I could not unravel the yarn he was spinning and began to get needled, but knitting my eyebrows I finally pinned him down and made him stop pulling the wool over my eyes and stringing me along. After that I managed to follow the thread better and he soon had me in stitches with his dyed in the wool homespun philosophy'. *To be on tenterhooks* is also from this source. One must be cautious though – neither *warp* as in 'warped sense of humour' nor *loom* as in 'loom large' have anything to do with weaving. The passage from Whitney quoted in Chapter 1 (see pp. 12–13) noted several less obvious usages of terms incorporating the *plex* root which belongs here, as does *to ply*.

I leave the reader to consider the contributions of chemistry (*quintessential, sublime, refined, ferment,* and *precipitate* ...), steam engines (*go off the rails, let off steam, side-track, shunt...*), electricity (*get your wires crossed, plug in, on the same wavelength, blow a fuse...*), and the more traditional realms of horse-control (*to rein in, to spur on, to break in, to change horses in midstream* ...), building (*to lay a firm foundation, to buttress...*), and so on. They might also ponder on *ponderous,* rummage around for the origin of *rummage,* and consider if the meaning of *encapsulate* can be otherwise encapsulated.

Before finishing this chapter there is another type of source with which we should deal: proper names. Usually a specific individual cannot be used as a public referent for maintaining word-meaning for two reasons: first, they are not known to everybody using the language, and are in any case mortal; and second, perhaps more profoundly, because consensus on their personality and qualities is unlikely to be universal. We have, as William James said (1890:Ch. X), as many selves as there are people who know us. Occasionally there are exceptions: 'Christian', and 'Buddhist' perhaps come closest to incorporating the total personality of their source into their meaning. More typically some salient aspect of the individual is identified: their philosophy of life (Confucian, Machiavellian, Platonic), scientific theory (Darwinian, Marxist, Freudian), or style (Wildean, Byronic)[4].

In order to keep this chapter to a manageable scale I have had to omit from the discussion many PL sources, some of which really do deserve a fuller examination. Table 3.3 provides a provisional summary of the major sources.

The function of this chapter has been principally to raise to consciousness how systematically and thoroughly our public worlds – the worlds of natural phenomena, the human body, our overt behaviour, our artefacts, and our visible social institutions –

Table 3.3   Major sources of Psychological Language

Source		Examples
Natural	1. Basic sensory phenomena and properties	hard, hot, bright, rough, sharp, bent, straight
	2. Human body	hearty, nosy, handy, to bellyache
	3. Basic motor behaviour	to see, to look, handle, to hold, to stamp on
	4. General behaviour	to follow, to turn to, to fix, to lose, to give
	5. Spatio-temporal relationships	high, down, superior, underlying, distant
	6. Classes of physical objects	
	a) animals	(*see text*)
	b) weather/climate	under the weather, frosty, stormy, windy, breezy
	c) plants	branch out, get to the root of, blossoming, rosy
	d) other	stony, abysmal, on rocky ground, to swamp, muddy
	7. Behaviour of physical objects and physical processes	(animal behaviour terms — *see text*), drained, wilting, crumbling, to evaporate
	8. Biologically based social roles (pre-dating language)	maternal, fraternal, paternal, sisterly, childish
Cultural	9. Social roles	regal, slavish, bourgeois matronly, magisterial
	10. Role/craft behaviours	to hunt, to preach, monkish, to hawk, wizardry
	11. Paradigm persons	Christian, Machiavellian
	12. Complex behaviour related to crafts etc.	to sew up, to brew, to weave, to steer, to reap
	13. Phenomena associated with 12.	(*see cooking terms in text*)
	14. Scientific/technological terms	to refine, to program, to distil, run out of steam, out of gear
	15. Complex belief systems	pious, holy, karma, faith

Note: boundaries between some of these are blurred and the above classification is not intended to be definitive in any sense. Discussion of category 15 is deferred until Chapter 5.

have been incorporated into the PL with which we think about ourselves. To some extent this may seem to be spelling out the obvious, but what does emerge surely is the complexity of each of these sources once we begin to examine it more closely – the role of 'seeing' and 'light', for example, or a craft like cooking. I believe it cannot be stressed too strongly that our current repertoire of psychological concepts and ideas is the cumulative legacy of millennia of human activities, of, in a sense, learning lessons about ourselves, especially from the physical world. The treatises of philosophers, theologians and indeed psychologists are built on this basis, on the anonymous labours of generations of carpenters, sailors, farmers, weavers, wives, and smiths. Such a perspective is not incompatible with the Marxist position that consciousness is a product of social relations (Sève 1978) but does suggest that the orthodox Marxist focus on *contemporary* social relations may be misleading. In the first place the centrality of basic sensory and behavioural terms implies the existence of a fairly universal psychological core which would be relatively unaffected by current social structure, and secondly the temporal inertia of the PL vocabulary means the retention of schemata dating from earlier historical periods when social structure and economic relations were other than they are at present.

CHAPTER FOUR

PHYSIOMORPHISM AND THE HISTORY OF PSYCHOLOGY

Studies in the history of Psychology have advanced considerably since the mid-1970s. The perspectives and insights of contemporary history of science have been incorporated, and traditional 'Whiggish' and 'internalist' approaches largely left behind. Welcome as such developments are, there are nevertheless some fundamental questions which have not been seriously confronted. In our eagerness to prove we are good members of the history of science club, we have continued to dodge the ever-vexed question of the scientific status of Psychology. Instead, our adherence to the post-positivist perspectives of history of science has served only to further legitimate the 'scientific' status of Psychology (Richards 1987a). The interpretation of PL that has been proposed in the previous chapters suggests a new angle from which to view the history of Psychology, one which immediately compels us to look at the 'status of Psychology' question afresh. While it would be inappropriate in the present work to consider the history of Psychology at length, the present chapter will be concerned with illustrating how the physiomorphic interpretation of PL may shed new light on the topic.[1]

THE STATUS OF PSYCHOLOGY

The status of Psychology has been problematical ever since the seventeenth Century. Indeed, Ross (1988) makes it clear that the very concept of 'consciousness' was not clearly formulated until Locke, and that in neither Descartes nor Hobbes do we find a term which genuinely corresponds to it. In an important respect

Psychology's troubles do, though, appear to lie in Descartes' restriction of the realm of mechanistic explanation to material phenomena, excluding by fiat the very notion of a science of Mind. Rejected almost immediately by Hobbes, this issue has haunted Psychology ever since. Either psychologists adhere diligently to what they take to be the canons of good scientific method and produce accounts which most people feel to be devoid of profundity and dehumanizingly reductionist, or they attempt to address the profounder issues and find themselves damned as unscientific. Sometimes, as with Freud, they are damned as both reductionist *and* unscientific, but these are complex cases. The taboo on attempting to create a 'Science of Mind' effectively persisted until the mid-nineteenth century, although numerous philosophers sympathetic to science endeavoured to study the mind in a way which was consistent with the scientific spirit (Herbart, Lotze, and James Mill for instance).

Closer examination of the seventeenth-century situation in Britain reveals that it was not just the Cartesian move which was the inhibiting factor but a deeply-rooted notion of the nature of language itself. The initial curious feature of the situation is that, far from having expanded by assimilating the WL novelties generated by the Scientific Revolution, the PL vocabulary drawn on by Locke (1689; rep. 1964) in treating psychological issues had become, on the face of it, considerably impoverished by comparison with, for example, Robert Burton's *Anatomy of Melancholy* (1624; rep. 1986). This shift warrants closer scrutiny. Taking Burton and Locke as our points of reference, the difference signifies a quite radical change in approach to the exploration of the psychological. This is not simply a matter of different literary styles or personality; a transposition of their temporal order would involve a glaring psychological anachronism. Their different approaches to the psychological as a topic for enquiry betray a profound difference in their own psychologies – a difference not simply of individual temperament but between the epochs in which they flourished. This is a specific instance of the rise of what Reiss (1982) has called 'analytico-referential discourse'. We have moved from a divergent synthetic literary orientation to a convergent analytic 'scientific' one, and this move is not merely a matter of method – it also carries its own psychological consequences.

If, though, we turn to contemporary views of language, the reasons for this apparent impoverishment of PL become somewhat clearer. This involves us in a slight detour into one of the currently more obscure preoccupations of mid-seventeenth century British Natural Philosophers: their fascination with the revision of language. The major figures here are Hobbes himself, and John Wilkins, who in 1668 published *An Essay Towards a Real Character and a Philosophical Language*. Wilkins was no marginal figure: he was a founding member of the Royal Society, an associate of Hartlib, Sprat, and Ward, and in the year his book appeared became Bishop of Chester. While space does not permit any detailed treatment of this episode (see T. Davies 1987 for a fuller account), the thrust of the argument was a need to rid language of what Hobbes called "metaphors, and senseless and ambiguous words", but as Davies says:

> while Hobbes only grumbles about the semantic treacherousness of natural language...Wilkins aspires...to abolish language altogether and to replace it with a *"Real Universal Character*, that should not signifie *words* but *things* and *notions"*, thus inverting the traditional relation between speech and writing
>
> (1987:86–7)

Wilkins was fascinated by the notion that in the original language (Hebrew in his view) there was no distinction between words and things – every word signified precisely one thing and misunderstanding between speakers was impossible. (This kind of thinking is the target of Swift's satire in the Laputan episode of *Gulliver's Travels* (1726–7: Part III, Chapter 5) where 'many of the most Learned and Wise adhere to the new Scheme of expressing themselves by *Things*', which, whilst having the disadvantage of requiring 'Sages' to carry great bundles of things upon their backs, had the advantage that 'it would serve as an universal Language to be understood by all civiliz'd Nations'.) To, as it were, redeem the curse of Babel, language must be reconstructed to directly and unambiguously reflect the Universe. This task in turn would require, to quote Davies again, 'the "just enumeration" and systematic classification of *everything in the universe*...along with all their parts, attributes and relations.' (1987:87) – a task Wilkins entered into with gusto. But note also the second point in the passage quoted above – the implicit primacy of writing over the spoken word. (Are we are here at the birth of Popper's 'World Three', the world of 'objective knowledge'?)

Although Wilkins' work represents the most extreme statement of this attitude to language it expressed a mood widespread among British Natural Philosophers, a mood which was a logical consequence of their impatience with the mystifying, multivalent, language of their predecessors. And among those sharing the mood, if not Wilkins' analysis, was Locke himself, who sought to demonstrate in Book III of the *Essay* how words, which for him signified ideas, derived ultimately from ideas of sensation, and who fulminated against rhetoric (see Bennington 1987). The implication of this for our present concern should now be fairly obvious: by eschewing metaphor and ambiguity and seeking to render language – philosophical language anyway – a straight univalent reflection of the world of referents, the Natural Philosophers of the Restoration had cut the ground of PL generation from under their own feet. In post-Wittgensteinian retrospect it is easy to see that they radically misunderstood the very nature of language, but in historical context their move is readily comprehensible, and was in some respects a distant anticipation of Logical Positivist aspirations to clarify the nature of knowledge by cutting the metaphysical cackle.

Such a philosophical programme was doomed to failure, but does, I believe, explain why overtly psychological thought in the wake of the Scientific Revolution did *not* draw extensively on the numerous discoveries of the period to formulate theories and models of psychological processes. Yet if the front door was closed the back door was open, and what was kept at bay by metaphor-phobic philosophers was eagerly seized on by physiologists wrestling to make mechanical sense of enigmatic flesh. And from thinking about the body in a new way to experiencing it in a new way is barely a single step.

Having said all that, Natural Philosophy had made an impact on philosophical PL in one important respect. The twin notions of mechanism and atomism had very deeply affected the way in which psychological matters were conceptualized. The first of these effectively makes its British debut in Hobbes, notably in his accounts of thinking and perception, while his discussion (1651)

'Of Imagination', Chapter 2 of *Leviathan*, begins with an affirmation of the Galilean concept of inertia – '..that when a thing is in motion it will eternally be in motion, unless somewhat else stay it' – which serves to underpin the subsequent account of all imagination and memory as 'decaying sense'. (May Hobbes's psychology be construed as not only physiomorphically assimilating the Cartesian concept of mechanism, but of Galileo's inertia too, as a necessary basis for properly conceptualizing the nature of this mechanism?) It may also be seen in the way in which the meaning of the physiological concept of 'animal spirits' changes even though the expression itself persists. In the earlier part of the century, 'animal spirits' refers to something vaguely metaphysical, a sort of mental fluid or perhaps a life-force, travelling through the nerves and blood-vessels. In Descartes' *Passions of the Soul* (1650), they have become formed only by 'very subtle parts of the blood' and 'are nothing but material bodies...of extreme minuteness' (Article X). By the time Pordage is translating Thomas Willis (1681) into English this mechanistic move has gone still further.[2] Willis though, while conceding that atomistic approaches have succeeded in solving several difficulties, believes that they bring in concepts 'too far removed from senses', and adopts as his central explanatory principles chemical, rather than mechanical, processes. Of these, 'fermentation' constitutes the most important. As Nakamura (1977) puts it, 'To Willis a living body was an entity which might be compared to a chemical laboratory or brewing factory provided with ferments, reagents, and chemical apparatus' (1977: 31). He provides detailed accounts in his works on the brain and on fermentation (Willis 1681, 1684) of how animal spirits are distilled from the blood, and how they are distributed via the blood-vessels in the brain:

> If it be inquired into, what benefit its Turnings and
> Convolutions afford to the brain, or for what its whole
> anfractuous or broken crankling frame is, we say, that the
> brain is so framed, both for the more plentiful reception of
> the spiritous aliment, and also for the more commodious
> dispensation of the animal Spirits for some uses.
>
> (1681:92)

The inertia of the expression 'animal spirits' throughout the century masks a shift in the framework of medical thinking from the Galenian to the mechanistic and chemical.[3]

Romanyshyn (1982) has reflected at length on the psychological consequences of Harvey's discovery in 1628 of the circulation of the blood and the demotion of the heart to the function of a pump, an issue first raised by Hill (1964) and Whitteridge (1971) (see also Webster (ed.) 1974). This organ, so rich in symbolic significance, so central to much traditional thought on the relation between body and mind and the nature of the emotions, is radically demystified, and with the demystification comes a separation between the 'real, factual, empirical and/or literal' heart-as-pump and the 'unreal, fictional, psychological, and/or metaphorical' heart (Romanyshyn, 1982:109). Oblivious of the caveats of Descartes' own dualism, the British philosophers and their associates in physiology proceed in quest of mental mechanisms and picture psychological processes in mechanical terms. Thus Locke (an erstwhile student of Willis's incidently) can write of memories being 'roused and tumbled out of their dark cells into open daylight by some turbulent and tempestuous passion' (1689; reprinted 1964:II.10.vii), (how different from St Augustine's 'vast cloisters of my memory'!) and a little earlier:

> the constitution of the body does sometimes influence the memory; since we oftentimes find a disease quite strip the mind of all its ideas, and the flames of a fever in a few days calcine all those images to dust and confusion, which seemed to be as lasting as if graved in marble.
>
> (II.10.v)

In general though, Locke reduces his mechanisms to the simplest and almost abstract terms; ideas come in trains, are compounded, divided, unite, or 'go constantly together'. Thus although there is a mechanistic *feel* to the *Essay* he relies primarily on a relatively restricted conventional vocabulary ('qualities', 'power', 'relations', etc.), which, however, he seeks to render more carefully technical and precise (e.g. as well as 'idea' itself his warnings about the term 'faculty' (II.21.vi) and apologetic redefinition of the term 'mode' (II.12.iv)). This, as noted above, is very different from the happy incorporation of newly discovered mechanisms and chemical processes into physiological thinking (Willis, for instance, comparing the brain to an alembic or writing of 'the ferment constituted in the chimney of the heart'). And can one fail to feel that there is some significance in the gradual replacement of the full-blooded term 'Passion' (from Lat. *passionem* = suffering, and having obvious religious resonances) by the anodyne 'Emotion' ('movement outwards')?[4]

The notion of atomism, closely linked to that of mechanism although not entirely synonymous with it, received its greatest impetus from the invention of the microscope. Whatever was placed beneath its lens proved to be corpuscular in nature – either comprised of cells, like vegetable tissue or insect wings, or minute machinery, like the flea. This astonishing revelation of the microscopic scale on which Nature ultimately organized the material world (most famously in Hooke's *Micrographia*, 1665) could have but one consequence for psychological thinkers living in the social and intellectual milieu of Natural Philosophy – that an understanding of the mind must similarly require an analysis into quasi-atomic components. In Locke this finds its most eminent advocate. Mind is comprised of quasi-atomic ideas, and at their heart, the building blocks of all experience, lie the 'ideas of sensation'. But in the history of science nothing is simple; Locke's own attitude to the value of the microscope was distinctly ambivalent. The psychological impact of the microscope as such was indeed surprisingly complex. To many (particularly in the area of medicine) it seemed a trivial pursuit unable to reveal anything of use or value – and Locke shared some of these doubts. To others it was a key instrument in the refutation of older doctrines of occult essences, 'signatures', and 'powers', translating these from the metaphysical into the physical (see Wilson 1988). And was one looking at this world in more detail or into a different world entirely? As Wilson points out, the empiricist view that knowledge was obtained through the senses meant, to some of its adherents, through the *unaided* senses. The extent to which British Natural Philosophers did in fact share a clearly formulated 'mechanical philosophy' during the latter seventeenth century is currently a matter of considerable debate, and mechanistic positions, which saw matter as passive and acted upon by motion originating externally (ultimately from God), cannot be fully equated to materialist positions in general (where Willis properly belongs, in which matter could itself be active) – of which they are strictly speaking but a subset. The picture I have painted here of a steady advance over the century of a coherent mechanistic-atomistic-materialist world-view is in truth a very crude characterization of a most intellectually complex period, but it must suffice for present purposes.

There is much more to be said about this period: the rising speculations about whether human nature stripped of civilized trappings was good (Winstanley 1652) or bad (Hobbes 1651)[5], and Puritan Psychology (as exemplified in Bunyan's *Pilgrim's Progress*), being but two topics deserving further attention. But we must return to the 'Status of Psychology' question.

We can already in the seventeenth century discern the first stirrings of a process which was to slowly gather momentum over the next two centuries. As scientists discover more about the world, and as the terms of their discoveries acquire a more specialized and technical character, so the physiomorphic assimilation of these ceases to be a matter, as hitherto, for the linguistic community as a whole. It comes instead to require the services of thinkers capable of understanding the nature of these increasingly arcane scientific findings. To put it briefly, Psychology arose, I believe, as an institutionalization of the physiomorphic process, a move arising from the increasingly technical character of the WL changes which fuel that process. At a slightly different level, the psychological gulf between Burton and Locke may itself be construed as stemming from the physiomorphic assimilation of 'Natural Philosophical behaviour'; that is to say, disciplined and systematic 'knowledge-gaining' as a mode of behaving vis-à-vis the external world resulted in the psychological being experienced in epistemological terms. To understand the mind is equivalent to understanding the process of understanding; knowledge of the mind is ultimately knowledge about how knowledge is acquired. The philosopher is experiencing himself (women do not seem to figure in all this in the seventeenth century!) *as* a knowledge-gaining being. The moral imperative to goodness, the life of the 'Passions', the social imperative to 'Honour', and creative, artistic, celebration of the cosmos become subsidiary psychological functions. To be anachronistic, psychology is, for the British Empiricists, primarily a matter of information processing. And this very move is a species of physiomorphic assimilation, assimilation of a new *behaviour* – scientific behaviour. This underwrites much subsequent use by psychological writers of specific products of scientific enquiry, and never more so than in modern cognitive Psychology.

To sum up: Psychology has its roots in the need for an institutionalization of the physiomorphic process vis-à-vis the WL generated by Natural Philosophical enquiry. But in identifying with the Natural Philosophical world-view, those engaged in this see the realm of the psychological as itself centrally epistemological. Thus a large and central part of all future Psychological thought is going to be about the efficacy of WL-encoded scientific discoveries not just as models of psychological processes *per se*, but as models of *epistemological* processes.

In the remainder of this chapter I will consider, albeit fairly briefly, a number of questions in the history of Psychology to which I believe a physiomorphic account offers some illuminating answers.

WHAT WAS MESMERISM ABOUT?

The period between the seventeenth century and the emergence of Psychology in the mid-nineteenth century is far from barren of psychological thought; on the contrary, a cataloguing of proto-Psychological work during this period would be extensive, ranging from social philosophers such as Rousseau to Gall's Phrenology. Rose (1985) has argued cogently for Itard's (1801) study of Victor, 'The Wild Boy of Aveyron', (see Lane 1979) as marking the first opening of a space for a genuinely psychological realm of study, it hitherto being assimilated either into physiology (e.g. the work on reflexes by Haller, Whytt, and Prochaska (see Danziger 1983; French 1969)) or philosophy (Hartley, Hume, Kant, Stewart, etc.). This analysis is I think consistent with what has been said above regarding the situation at the end of the seventeenth century.[6] Among these proto-Psychological episodes, Mesmerism is particularly pertinent to the present theme as it illustrates with unusual clarity the impact of novel scientific discovery on psychology (in the subject matter sense) and the felt need to mediate this impact in an ostensibly scientific fashion.

The term 'electrifying' was coined by Franklin in 1747; a mere five years later the OED records the first PL usage 'to startle, rouse, excite, as though with the shock of electricity' (OED 2):

> 'You will not be so agreeably electrified as you were at Manheim' (from Chesterfield's *Letters*)

Barely recognized in the seventeenth century, electrical phenomena and the concept of electricity rapidly became one of the leading enigmas confronting eighteenth century science. Fire was puzzling enough, but invisible, elusive, shocking, electricity far surpassed it. Its properties harked back to the unseen rays and occult forces of the Hermeticists and Paracelsians. But its reality was vouchsafed by the most materialist of scientific thinkers. While the Cavendishes and Coulombs wrestled with the rival merits of corpuscular and mathematical conceptualizations of the 'imponderable' (i.e. 'weightless') electrical fluid (or fluids), and their laboratories filled with awesome Leyden jars and 'fulminating plates', the general public perhaps began to feel for the first time a sensation with which we are now all too familiar – experts operating beyond our ken have unleashed something nobody understands and let's keep our fingers crossed. But it was exciting too. An occult force with the imprimatur of scientific respectability, it reopened the door on the possibility of strange and intimate cosmic interconnections which sensible levers-and-cogs mechanism had seemed to exclude. It is in this context that we need to consider Mesmer's notion of 'Animal Magnetism'. From the viewpoint being adopted here, the episode represents the physiomorphic assimilation of novel electrical phenomena. Quite literally we are to think of ourselves as emanating, conducting, and storing a form of magnetic energy. Mesmer's starting point was the postulation of a

> fluid universally diffused, and so continuous as not to admit
> of any vacuum, and the subtlety of which does not allow of
> any comparison, and which by its nature is capable of
> receiving, propagating, and communicating all impulses
>
> (Harte 1902:16)

this being the vehicle of a 'reciprocal influence between the heavenly bodies, the earth and animated bodies' (*ibid*:15). But while this sounds as if it verges on the mystical, the reciprocal action is nevertheless 'governed by mechanical laws, at present unknown' (*ibid*:16). He then proceeds, in Propositions IX and X of the twenty seven from which I have been quoting to state:

> IX. Properties similar to those of the magnet are found in the human body; different and opposite poles can be distinguished, which can be excited, changed, destroyed, or reinforced; even the phenomenon of inclination is observed in it.
> X. The property of the animal body, which makes it susceptible to the influence of the heavenly bodies, and to the reciprocal action of those that surround it, has led me, from its analogy with the magnet, to call it Animal Magnetism.
>
> (Harte 1902:16)

The electricity and magnetism (the relationship between which was at that time still obscure) studied by contemporary science were also related to this more ether-like universal fluid, although how precisely is not made clear. Mesmer claims, though, that

> XXI. This system will furnish new ideas about the nature of fire and light, and throw light upon the theory of attraction [i.e. gravity], of flux and reflux, of the magnet, and of electricity.
>
> (Harte 1902:17).

The most telling quotation however comes from Puységur, Mesmer's leading disciple:

> M. Mesmer has often said to those who could understand it, that in his natural state a man has poles, and an equator, and is in a magnetised state naturally; but that the aim of Animal Magnetism is to put him on a pivot, for then a man at once presents the same phenomena as a magnetised bar of iron, also on its pivot. A man in his normal state can be compared to the needle of a compass which has been taken off its pivot and laid on the table. If you lay it on the table it will certainly not cease to be magnetised; but until you replace it on its pivot it will not take any particular direction.
>
> (Harte 1902:23)

Mesmer's goals were therapeutic ones. He sought to cure by bringing the flow of the magnetic fluid in the individual back into natural harmony with its cosmic flow. I am not concerned here with giving an account of Mesmer's career.[7] What I wish to draw attention to is that he was involved in trying to systematically explore the implications of construing human nature in terms of the electrical phenomena, particularly magnetism, fascinating his contemporaries in the physical sciences. Having learned to experience themselves in terms of chemical and hydraulic phenomena, as complex conduits of animal spirits, rarefying and condensing vapours, cooling and overheating blood, people are now to think of themselves as magnets, between whom invisible streams of animal magnetism constantly flow. Subject to the therapeutic attentions of the Mesmerist they are placed like compass-needles on a pivot where they can presumably swing back to the True North of their physiological being and properly align themselves in the curative flows of the universal fluid, which emanates ultimately from God. It is like a more pious version of W. Reich's 'orgone'.

How at this remove we are to evaluate the scenes of collective hysteria-cum-Primal Therapy around the famous *baquet* in Mesmer's Parisian salon, or the even weirder scenes attending his visit in 1775 to the baronial castle of the Hungarian Baron Hareczky I am at a complete loss to say. Seyfert's account of the latter in Harte (1902:34-42) is at once so baffling and so hilarious that only Roger Corman and Vincent Price in their prime could do cinematic justice to it. (Somewhat similar, if less theatrical, scenes appear to have attended T. S. Hall's (1843) lectures on Phreno-Magnetism in English provincial towns in the 1840s.) My principle point is that the appearance on the scene of something like Mesmer's doctrine of Animal Magnetism is precisely what one would predict in the light of the physiomorphic account – a phenomenon of a new kind in the external world will inevitably bring novel psychological ideas in its wake.[8] It may be objected that Mesmer's ideas were physiological, not psychological, but the fact is that we can now be mesmerized by magnetic personalities and sometimes encounter people who are our polar opposites. And although the PL term *attractive* had long been in use, the notion of Animal Magnetism surely gave it an added connotation in such expressions as 'they felt strangely attracted to one another'. As observed earlier, it is via accounts of the physiological that science-derived PL changes during this period were most readily effected. The passage from Puységur cited above makes it quite explicit: for Mesmer we were magnets. And if you believe you are a magnet you will construe your experience accordingly.

WHY FREUD WON'T LIE DOWN

There can be little doubt that in terms of direct impact on PL, Psychoanalytic theory has been more influential than any other school of Psychological thought. We project, repress, regress, make Freudian slips, accept that we may have unconscious reasons for doing things, search for father- and mother-figures, have Oedipus complexes, see things as phallic symbols, have fixations, defend our egos, obey (or not) our superegos, suffer from Death-wishes, and feel our libidos rising. If we are only slightly more acquainted with psychoanalytic jargon we may also find ourselves describing people as anal characters, orally dependent or aggressive, engaging in reaction-formation, or sublimating their anxieties in a creative fashion. This is especially frustrating to people like H. J. Eysenck whose four-decade-long attack on Freud, psychoanalysis, and all who sail in it, bears all the hallmarks of an obsessional repetition neurosis rooted in a patricidal fantasy of killing off the disciplinary father-figure whom he has striven so hard to replace. But knowing one's EPI score will never seriously rival Oedipal regression as an exciting route to self-knowledge. At the 1987 British Psychological Society Conference I saw on the Penguin bookstand a copy of Eysenck's final anti-Freudian fling *The Decline and Fall of the Freudian Empire* (1986); above it were two shelves-full of the latest Penguin edition of Freud's works. Will Eysenck's works still be so prominent fifty years after his death?

This is not meant as gratuitous Eysenck-bashing. Discovering many years ago that my EPI score fell on the dot labelled 'disthymic' did wonders for me. The issue it points to is that in spite of decades of very powerful and cogent attacks on the scientific calibre of Freud's own research and the coherence of psychoanalytic theory, plus arguments *ad hominem ad nauseam*, plus, too, the fact that by all accounts a theory formulated for the most part prior to 1930 should by now be obsolete in the normal run of things, Psychoanalysis will not lie down. And Eysenck's latest report of its death is as exaggerated as all previous reports to that effect. The situation obviously requires diagnosis. What is it about Freudian theory that enables it to retain its appeal in the face of perennial criticism and refutation?

One clue to this lies in David Rapaport's 1959 essay 'The structure of Psychoanalytic theory: a systematizing attempt'. In his introductory section Rapaport addresses three issues: a) the influences on Freud, b) the levels of analysis at which Psychoanalysis operates, and c) his underlying models. As regards the influences we are immediately struck by their range, which extends beyond his immediate neurological and psychiatric training to a wide knowledge of literature, the Jewish tradition (an influence later explored further by Bakan (1975)), and Brentano's 'act psychology'. This is underpinned by a commitment to thoroughgoing determinism derived from Helmholtz. Regarding levels of analysis, Rapaport concludes that by the time it was fully developed:

> A system of multiple levels of analysis evolves, including the
> dynamic, economic, structural, genetic, and adaptive levels,
> whose foundations had already been built in the earlier
> phases... psychoanalytic theory, by its conception of "over-
> determination", kept itself open to all relevant "levels of
> analysis," and was not limited to a single one as were many
> other theories.

(1959:19-20)

Finally, and crucially for us, Rapaport identifies four 'distinct models' which Freud incorporates: the 'Reflex-Arc (or Topographic) Model', the 'Entropy (or Economic) Model', the 'Darwinian (or Genetic) Model', and the 'Jacksonian (or Neural Integration Hierarchy) Model'.

The initial picture then is of the young Freud casting his intellectual net extremely widely across nineteenth-century scientific thought, drawing in not only the most advanced ideas about neurology but also evolutionary thought and a broadly positivist concept of scientific explanation: scientific explanations are to be couched ultimately in terms of the distribution of a single kind of physical energy governed by the laws of thermodynamics (hence the 'entropy' component in his thinking). In his

Psychoanalytic theory these are then synthesized into a single, if extremely complex, multi-level, image of human nature. On this basis we can provisionally suggest that the reason for the extraordinary resilience of Psychoanalysis is that Freud pre-empted all the key scientific metaphors of nineteenth-century science, forging from them the first truly 'modern' account of human nature. To construe one's psychological experience in Freudian terms was to engage in a wholesale physiomorphic assimilation of the nineteenth-century scientific universe. Insofar as this is in many fundamental respects still with us, subsequent Psychological thought has been unable to outflank it.

But this is not the whole story. Psychoanalysis as a therapeutic and self-exploratory procedure provided a route by which the mapping of psychological experience in these terms could be undertaken by the individual. Since some key features of this procedure such as dream-analysis, free-association, and the like were widely described in psychoanalytic literature one did not have to actually be in analysis to undertake at least preliminary Freudian forays into one's unconscious. Psychoanalysis provided not only a radical extension of PL but a way of obtaining the new experiences to which that PL refered. Indeed it *created* these experiences. When further account is taken of Freud's virtuosity with metaphors of all kinds as a literary technique for expounding his ideas the force of his vision becomes even clearer. In this respect it is enlightening to contrast him with his near-contemporary William James, another master of metaphor. In the *Principles of Psychology* (1890), James too incorporates nineteenth-century WL into the psychologist's repertoire; the evolutionary perspective is there, while 'submaximal nerve-irritations', 'telephone-plates', kaleidoscopes, buried electrodes, 'associational brain-tracts', and 'irradiations' pepper his account of the Stream of Thought (Chapter X) along with hosts of metaphors and images of a more poetic kind. But James's goal is different from Freud's. James is striving for phenomenological evocation, for the reader's 'shock of recognition' of the accuracy of his description of familiar psychological phenomena and of such elusive experiences as tip-of-the-tongue phenomena and the struggle to recall a momentarily lost name. To this end the way his metaphorical passages work is to lay down a barrage of images in order to convey the quality of the phenomenon in question (e.g. the character of the 'transitive' passages of thought). As heir to the New England Transcendentalist tradition of Thoreau and Emerson (who dandled him on his knee as a child) James is too good a writer for this to be described as a hit-and-miss procedure – his metaphors are nearly all hits – but in the end he tells us nothing new, only reflects with considerable brilliance what we knew already.

Freud's strategy is quite different. His figurative passages are very carefully-deployed and calculated exercises in rendering the novel comprehensible; they are explanatory, not evocative. In the first of his *Five Lectures on Psycho-Analysis* (1910, trans. 1957) for example, where he is addressing his assembled disciplinary peers (probably including James) at Clark University, he has to explain the notion that people can suffer from their memories of which hysterical symptoms are 'mnemic symbols'. In a passage too long to quote in full he compares these symbols to Charing Cross and the Monument in London, then proceeds:

> But what would we think of a Londoner who paused today in deep melancholy before the memorial of Queen Eleanor's funeral instead of going about his business in the hurry that modern working conditions demand or instead of feeling joy over the youthful queen of his own heart? Or again what should we think of a Londoner who shed tears before the Monument that commemorates the reduction of his beloved metropolis to ashes although it has long since risen again in far greater brilliance? Yet every single hysteric and neurotic behaves like these two impractical Londoners.
>
> (1901:16-17)

The listener is carefully guided to a new insight, or at least given the impression that they have been. The strength of Freud's Psychology then rests, first, on the fact that the underlying models he is using encompass the central concepts dominating contemporary science; second, that he provides a method of creating the psychological experiences which realize (in the literal sense of making real) these models; and, third, that in his writings he has a sufficient mastery of the use of language to plausibly guide, educate, and persuade the reader into adopting his perspective. The new PL generated by Psychoanalysis succeeds in large part by virtue of the added depth of meaning given to terms like projection, repression, complex, and fixation. This is achieved because of our prior persuasion that we should think of psychic life as an energy-distribution system developing over time and involving the interrelationships between a conscious Ego, an unconscious Id, and a Superego (these latter technical terms being translations from less technical-sounding German originals). And to think of our psychic life in this way is, in a fundamental sense, to incorporate within ourselves the principles governing the nineteenth-century scientific universe.

But what of the so far missing Hamlet in this account – sex? The key which gains access to those experiences which validate the psychoanalytic account is the 'discovery' that sexual energy is the fundamental psychological form which energy (of which there is really only one variety) takes. And here there is a curious echo of Mesmer – in discovering within oneself the primacy of the sexual is one not thereby enabled to align oneself with the energy flow of the universe just as successful Mesmeric treatment aligned one in harmony with the flowings of the imponderable universal fluid? Perhaps this is going too far. What is less disputable is that in practice Psychoanalysis gave the impression of being energizing, of releasing energy within the individual which had been blocked or locked up, and that admission of the ultimately sexual nature of this energy was essential for its release. Healthy psychological life in these terms involves a full conscious acceptance of the 'psychic life as energy-distribution system' image.

I am not claiming here that this is all there is to be said about the reasons why Psychoanalysis has proved so immune to the slings and arrows of outraged psychologists and philosophers of science. What I am claiming is that the standpoint I have been advocating casts this immunity in a new light, for it suggests that what we have in Psychoanalysis is a comprehensive striving for the physio-morphic assimilation of the nineteenth-century scientific universe – evolutionary, entropic, deterministic, reducible to patterns of energy distribution, and, in physiology, espousing a hierarchical model of neurological organization broadly reflecting the various levels of evolutionary 'progress'. This, for Freud, is what humans are. Within this framework subsidiary psychological mechanisms analogous to chemical processes (e.g. sublimation), archaeological excavation, and even classical economics can be readily incorporated. We are no longer living entirely in Freud's universe; Einstein's Theory of Relativity, the Big Bang theory, and computers have seen to that. But we have not abandoned it entirely either, and some of its central features remain fairly secure. Until these too are surpassed, Psychoanalytic thought will continue to speak to us.

WHAT WAS WATSON'S ELEMENTARY MISTAKE?

If the PL fall-out of Psychoanalytic theory has permeated ordinary linguistic usage, J. B. Watson's original radical 'Behaviorism' has, in its own terms at any rate, barely left a mark. We may of course feel as if we've been conditioned, but this is a Pavlovian not Watsonian expression and, given its original meaning, is quite paradoxical since it was essentially not meant to refer to feelings at all but to a purely 'objective' relationship between particular behavioural responses and particular stimuli in a laboratory setting. More recent behaviour-modification approaches have begun to lend wider currency to 'reinforce', 'shaping', and 'schedule', but their cultural infiltration is slow. The impact of Watsonian Behaviorism was undoubtedly far-reaching but in retrospect looks primarily methodological in character. Certainly he placed learning theory at the centre of US experimental practice, but his most influential behaviourist successors all in their various ways parted company with his own initial formulation of Behaviorist doctrine. Much of his writing now reads as extremely dated (by contrast with James, Freud, and such contemporary British writers as Stout, Ward, and Rivers) and, especially when he writes about child-rearing, one can respond with little else than a gleefully derisive hoot; on why mothers 'coddle' their children:

her own whole being cries out for the expression of love. Her mother before her has trained her to give and receive love. She is starved for love – affection, as she prefers to call it. It is at bottom a sex-seeking response in her, else she would never kiss the child on the lips. Certainly, to satisfy her professed reason for coddling, kissing the youngster on the forehead, on the back of the hand, patting it on the head once in a while, would be all the petting needed for a baby to learn that it is growing up in a kindly home.

(1928:80-1)

The problem with Watson's position goes deeper than his attitude to child-rearing however. It is quite clear from the tone that pervades his writings, from the 'manifesto' paper (Watson 1913) onwards, that his aspirations are radically iconoclastic. This is made explicit in the final paragraph of *Behaviorism* (1924; rep. 1970) where he urges a severance from 'legendary folk-lore of happenings thousands of years ago', and 'foolish customs and conventions which...hamper the individual like taut steel bands' (1970:303). And this aspiration has a linguistic dimension.

The central feature of Behaviorism is, famously, a refusal to endow subjective psychological phenomena with any scientific significance at all. Mentalistic language is to be rejected wholesale. It is to be replaced by an objective language for refering to overt behaviour. Only these phenomena are scientifically accessible, measurable, replicable, and subject to both experimental and practical control.[9] The problem for Watson, as R. S. Peters once observed regarding a much wider range of Psychological theories, was 'more...the desire to develop an ambitious theory than... puzzlement about concrete problems of human behaviour' (1964:1). He wanted to be *scientific*; it was not behaviour which puzzled him but how to study it *scientifically*. If mental phenomena were unamenable to scientific access then they could be discarded, to be replaced by behaviour, which was so amenable. (There are important 'externalist' dimensions to all this which need not immediately concern us.) It is here, from our current perspective, that we can locate his elementary mistake; as we have shown, the language of behaviour is intrinsically Janus-faced. One cannot label a behaviour 'touching', 'pointing', 'grasping', even 'moving' without at once creating a corresponding range of psychological phenomena. And this applies to 'conditioned' as well. To feel I have been conditioned is to feel that I have been subtly got at by someone else to behave in a way which I did not consciously intend. So the very notion that an 'objective' behaviour language carrying no 'mentalistic' connotations can somehow be devised by scientific fiat is mistaken. It runs counter to the whole way in which language operates, overlooking its central physiomorphic dynamic.

Even so, had this would-be objective behaviour language been generated in the course of trying to understand genuinely enigmatic behaviour, its input into PL might still have been considerable, regardless of Watson's attempts to constrain it within WL bounds. As it was it provided little but a detailed redescription of phenomena about which few people felt any deep bewilderment. The behaviourists' efforts were not entirely barren of effect, and in its later incarnations it has undoubtedly provided, for better or worse, at least the basis for a technology of behaviour-control. But is this not ultimately only a refinement of very ancient intuitions about the effects on behaviour of reward and punishment?

When it came to language itself Watson rapidly painted himself into a corner. Since language is a behaviour it is public and amenable to behaviourist study. But since the content of language consists in large part of talk about its users' mental lives how can the behaviourist sensibly construe it? Are all these speakers engaging in naive, unscientific, circumlocutory references to their behaviour? Or is there no more to being, for example, delighted than the fact that one says 'I am delighted?' And is even *thinking* that one is delighted only, as Watson claimed, 'subvocal speech' – detectable by sufficiently subtle instrumentation of the thinker's larynx? And what if she thinks it in French? And how would the French person's 'enchanté' differ from the English speaker's 'enchanted' on this criterion? The very existence of homophones demolishes the 'subvocal speech' theory of thought, while the Watsonian is bound to consider all PL use as gibberish, even while presumably being quite capable of understanding it when not writing scientific papers. Watson's own style is in fact highly emotional, though his theory has no room for such a phenomenon (e.g. his confession that 'I usually have to walk a block or two to let off steam' after witnessing a mother say 'Bless its little heart' when her child 'falls down, or stubs its toes, or suffers some other ill' (1928:82)).

The reality of a psychological realm is, as argued in Chapter 2, intrinsic to language. To try and restrict language to the WL mode is to misapprehend the very nature of language itself. Watson's blindness to this meant that his attempt to revolutionize our understanding of human nature by 'scientifically' compelling us to attend only to overt behaviour was bound to fail. The tradition he initiated within Psychology endured, it is true, but his successors had either to make fundamental concessions (like Tolman) or fell victim to the same paradoxes on an even grander scale (like Clark Hull). Skinner succeeded by avowedly eschewing any interest in theory whatsoever and concentrating on the technology; even so his appeal has become restricted. Beyond the confines of the discipline there is either ignorance and indifference to behaviourism, or wary suspicion, fear even, of the view of human life which it is perceived as entailing. It has certainly failed, in contrast to psychodynamic theories, to open out new realms of psychological meaning – bar one.

From the physiomorphic perspective then Watson's Psychology is the rule-proving exception. Precisely because he tried to reject PL he was unable to address any of the important *psychological* issues, while a WL language of behaviour devoid of a PL dimension can shed little on the behavioural issues either. But one, quite inadvertent, physiomorphic sequel, one 'new realm of psychological meaning', may nonetheless be discerned in the impact Behaviorism has had on Western psychology. This arises not from any theoretical doctrine but from the kind of research which widely epitomizes experimental Psychology and is inextricably identified with Watson. I refer of course to the maze-bound rat. We identify not with Watson but with his subjects. In the maze-bound rat we recognize, and are hence able to articulate, the condition of our existence in modern mass urban society. It is a world beyond our immediate control, a world the structure of which we can only blindly fathom by guess-work, a world organized by only dimly identifiable agencies who may change its rules apparently by whim; to many it is indeed a rat-race. It is not an environment in which inherited routines are likely to succeed but one which demands constant adaptation. 'Humans as rats' is not a flattering image but nevertheless it is one which in pessimistic moods we may recognize as only too applicable. Behaviourist rat research taught us to view rats as victims as well as vermin. The rat's relationship to the experimental psychologist became a symbol of the modern commoner's relationship to the scientific expert. Given Watson's Utopian goals this is peculiarly ironic. Whether this is accurate or fair or not to Behaviorism is in fact irrelevant – it remains a psychological fact that the principle cultural consequence of the movement was to implant a paranoid image in the popular mind of the existence of a body of scientific experts in behavioural manipulation who view us as maze-bound rats, thereby teaching us to view ourselves in the same terms. Not what Watson, aspiring guru on good parenting,[10] intended.

WAS GESTALT PSYCHOLOGY SCIENTIFIC?

Although English language histories of Psychology traditionally depict the scientific calibre of German Gestalt Psychology in a somewhat negative light in comparison with Behaviorism this would have surprised and puzzled its leading figures: Wertheimer the friend of Albert Einstein, and Kohler and Koffka, students of Stumpf and Max Planck at Berlin. Secure dwellers in the scientific heartland of European academia the question of their scientific *bona fides* would have never arisen. In spite of this, perhaps more accurately, because of it, they were fully sensitive to the problem of Psychology's scientific status. The way in which they attempted to resolve this problem was extremely subtle and brought them very close to the position adopted in the present work (the subtlety of which I do not judge). The key English text is Chapter 2 of Koffka's *Principles of Gestalt Psychology* (1935), entitled 'Behaviour and its Field'. While the argument is too complex for full presentation here it contains a central feature of interest to us in the present context, namely the key role taken by the concept of the 'psychological field' and the way in which this concept is introduced.

To set the scene: Koffka, having established the necessity of treating behaviour as molar rather than molecular, has made important distinctions between the 'geographical' and 'behavioural' environments and also between 'real', 'phenomenal', and 'apparent' behaviour. These preliminaries have provided the reader with a picture of the interrelationships logically obtaining between the physical world, the organism's behaviour, phenomenal experience, and the scientist who is trying to investigate this interacting system. Satisfied that 'we have laid the foundation for psychology as the science of molar behaviour', he continues:

We must now elaborate this point. Which are to be the most fundamental concepts of our system? One of the postulates of our psychology was that it be *scientific*. Therefore let us try to discover one of the fundamental concepts of science which we can apply to our task. A short excursion into the history of science will lead us to our discovery. How did Newton explain the motion of bodies?

(1935:41)

A rapid survey of the progress of the notion of 'fields' in physics ensues; it replaces 'action at a distance' until...

One fortress remained in the hands of the enemy, Newton's gravitation. In Einstein's theory of gravitation the actions at a distance disappeared just as they had disappeared before from electromagnetism, and the gravitational field took their place. Empty space as mere geometrical nothingness disappeared from physics, being replaced by a definitely distributed system of strains and stresses, gravitational and electromagnetic, which determines the very geometry of space. And the distribution of strains and stresses in a given environment will determine what a given constitution will do in that environment. Thus we discover the magnetic field of the earth by observing the behaviour of magnetic needles in different places. . . Thus the field and the behaviour of the body are correlative. Because the field determines the behaviour of bodies, this behaviour can be used as an indicator of the field properties. Behaviour of the body, to complete the argument, means not only its motion with regard to the field, it refers equally to the changes which the body will undergo; e.g. a piece of iron will become magnetized in a magnetic field.

(1935:42)

And then immediately to the crux of the matter:

Can we introduce the field concept into psychology, meaning by it a system of stresses and strains which will determine real behaviour? If we can, we have at once a general and scientific category for all our explanations and we should have the same two kinds of problems which the physicist encounters: viz, (1) what is the field at a given time, (2) what behaviour must result from a given field?

(1935:42)

In the wake of Einsteinian physics, a scientific Psychology must be couched in field-theoretical terms. The introduction of this 'psychological field' requires a reformulation of the earlier distinction between 'behavioural' and 'geographical' environment, for Koffka is reluctant on several counts to equate 'psychological field' to 'behavioural environment' in a simplistic fashion. The most significant of these for us is that he wishes to establish a 'unitary universe of discourse' in which we can talk about all levels of phenomena, thereby incorporating Psychology fully into the orbit of the physical sciences. Equating 'behavioural environment' and 'psychological field' would not fully achieve this for it would leave us still with one language for molar 'psychological' events and another for physical ones occuring in the 'geographical environment' in contrast to which the 'behavioural environment' was defined.

The Gestalt psychologists are not therefore merely latching onto 'field' as the latest scientific metaphor for the psychological but see it as the route by which scientific language in general can be unified, including the language of scientific Psychology, retaining its full literal scientific WL sense throughout. In trying to render this move coherent the principle difficulty is in bridging the psychology/physiology gulf. We seem to be faced with only two interacting 'material' fields – physics and physiology. How can the psychological be incorporated into this system? How can the notion of 'psychological field' be given the hard scientific meaning required rather than remaining just a figure of speech? To solve this, the second central concept of Gestalt Psychology is introduced – the notion of 'isomorphism' derived from topology, where it had been introduced in the late nineteenth century and subsequently used by physicists such as Poincaré. To try and simplify the ensuing complex argument without reducing it to incoherence: a) the physiological system has molar properties irreducible to those of its component parts, although these are little understood; b) these molar properties include, we *know*, consciousness or 'direct experience', and molar behaviour; c) the identifiable properties of this 'behavioural/psychological field' must be *isomorphic* with those of the physiological field which underlies them, i.e. the formal structure of events at the two levels *must* be the same – if this 'must' is denied we are driven into an unacceptable mind–body dualism; d) the 'psychological field' is therefore a molar structure in its own right; it is not, as the earlier 'behavioural environment' was, a *determinant* of psychological events; e) in studying the structure of this 'psychological field' we have a route for studying the obscure molar physiological processes with which it is – and has to be – isomorphic. The science of Psychology then is to be 'the study of behaviour in its causal connection with the psycho-physical field' (1935:67). In this way the scientific status of the discipline is salvaged and its scientific role made clear.

Looking back we can see a number of problems with Koffka's account, but there is no doubt that in this difficult and occasionally contradictory chapter he is attempting to confront and resolve the 'status of Psychology' question in a highly rigorous fashion; and in struggling to retain the scientific WL sense of 'field' he is explicitly acknowledging the existence of linguistic difficulties of the kind on which we are focusing. At the end of the day, though, it does seem that Psychology is as much the handmaiden of physiology as it is in Behaviorism, and it is unclear how such a conception of it can give Caesar, Shakespeare and Beethoven the 'same *outstanding* and *distinctive* position which they enjoy in the estimation of the ordinary educated person and the historian' (1935:27) – as he aspired to in the opening anti-behaviourist polemics.

In using the 'field' concept in the way just outlined Gestalt Psychology was aiming at nothing less than a *fusion* of the WL and PL levels of discourse. Their PL was not to be analogic, not a mere modelling, but was to refer directly to the psychological *reality*. In the event the programme failed. This chapter, one of the most important theoretical statements in the history of Psychology, is largely forgotten. Gestalt Psychology is remembered for Köhler's apes, its studies of visual illusions, some pioneer problem-solving experiments and perhaps Wertheimer's 'Little Gauss' anecdote.[11] The 'field' concept continued to be developed by psychologists such as Lewin and Smelser but it never acquired the theoretical centrality Koffka, Wertheimer, and Kohler wished, merely taking its place among the many other heuristically useful images in terms of which psychological theories may be couched. It is never-theless significant as the first serious attempt to incorporate a major twentieth-century physical science concept into Psychology following Freud's monopoly of nineteenth-century ones.

Was Gestalt Psychology scientific? The best answer is perhaps 'yes – too much so for its own good'.

THE HISTORY OF PSYCHOLOGY IN PHYSIOMORPHIC PERSPECTIVE

The four cases we have just been looking at are sufficient to indicate that the adoption of the physiomorphic perspective holds promise of shedding some new light on the nature of Psychology as revealed in its history. They lead me to propose the following:

a) Psychology, whatever else it is, constitutes an institution-alization of the normal process of physiomorphic assimilation of novel WL. This institutionalization being rendered necessary by the increasingly technical character of the novel WL being generated by the physical sciences.
b) A major WL innovation in the physical sciences will be followed by its incorporation into Psychological theorizing, particularly if it occurs in either the biological sciences or in information processing and data-storage technology.
c) The cultural success of such innovations is contingent upon their being able to provide new kinds of experience which endow them with phenomenological meaning. (This needs to be distinguished from some forms of within-discipline success where a highly specialized technical language may develop from the detailed exploration of a particular model – but ultimately I would be inclined to argue that assimilation into the cultural PL is the final test of the real value of a PL innovation.)

It must be stressed however that this is not meant by any means to be the whole story. The major missing dimension here is any consideration of the broader contextual issues such as the analysis of the 'Goals' or 'Social Interests' of Knowledge provided by the Critical Philosophy of Habermas and Apel and the socio-political conditions which determine the uses to which Psychology is put by its host societies. A deeper scrutiny would, I believe, reveal that the generation of new PL within Psychology by the physiomorphic process is a major mediator of these 'external' factors and embeds the discipline very firmly in its cultural contexts in a way not shared by the physical sciences – although they too can, it is agreed, be so embedded.

It must also be conceded that the dependency of Psychologists on ideas drawn from the physical sciences and technology has long been noted, but it has also tended to be a matter for lamentation. What is new in what I am saying is that given the nature of PL *it could not be any other way*. In recent decades the innovations have for the most part occured on three separate fronts. Firstly the rise of cognitive Psychology centring on advances in computer technology and information processing models. This retains the Lockean equation of the psychological and the epistemological. There are a number of reflexive twists in the logic of the use of computers to explore the psychological, not least the circularity of the fact that it was precisely to model some psychological processes that they were invented in the first place. This is not, though, the place to enter into the running battles on AI, on whether computers can think, and the precise extent to which the biological wetware is actually structured isomorphically with the programs for simulating it. From the present perspective a somewhat different thought arises: is the Psychologist who uses information technology language to characterize psychological processes doing anything fundamentally logically different from our predecessors who characterized them in terms of the most complex technologies or crafts of their day – weaving, clockwork, husbandry, or cooking, for example? Of course they are elaborating the analogy in far greater detail and take it seriously when a specific model couched in its terms breaks down (e.g. the demise of Collins' and Quillian's 1969 hierarchical model of verbal memory), but the underlying *continuity* of what they are doing with what we have always done needs to be equally stressed.

The second front is more clearly a continuation of older styles of physiomorphic assimilation: the study of animals. The great advances in our knowledge of animal behaviour brought about by ethology and comparative Psychology have had considerable psychological impact and genuinely enabled us to look at our own and other people's behaviour and experience in new ways. The first wave of ethological work by Lorenz, Tinbergen, and Eibl-Eibesfelt in the 1960s and early 70s[12] was almost subversive in the possibilities for debunking which it opened up: patriotism was stickleback territoriality (how *could* the Americans believe they would win in Vietnam?); military epaulettes were equivalent to the angry gorilla's raised shoulder hair; the boss's big desk and office were the top stag's mating ground; and advertisements were territorial markers differing in no essential respect from those left on lampposts by dogs; the rival bellowings of would-be dominant politicians had similar wildlife analogues. In short, quite a number of behaviours traditionally viewed as distinctively human and even embodying our finest civilized or spiritual qualities were revealed as embarrassingly similar to very uncivilized behaviours found throughout the animal kingdom, behaviours which served quite obvious functions and about which there was no mysterious spirituality at all. Even praying involved a typical primate submission gesture. The discovery of ourselves in animal behaviour is, as we saw in Chapter 3, one of the most anciently rooted forms of physiomorphism. Again then I am moved to ask, is what we are doing now any different? The familiar question 'how far can findings from animals be generalized to humans?' is perhaps misconceived. It assumes a static state of affairs with humans on the one side having a prefixed set of properties and animals on the other with their own similar sets – the question seeming to be simply the empirical one of 'do the two sets overlap in some respect?'. The physiomorphic view is a dynamic one – having identified a property in an animal do you want to add it to your set? Or is there a property in your existing set which corresponds to it? If the answer to the latter is yes, the situation is nonetheless altered, for the very identification of it with the animal property changes its psychological meaning – do you *still* want to be like that?

Thirdly, as ever, advances in physiological understanding have exerted a most direct and intimate effect on Psychology. We are perhaps in the middle of the most dramatic revolution in the psychological construal of our own bodies since the end of the seventeenth century. One finding in particular has had a wide cultural impact – the discovery of hemispheric differences in brain functioning. This has yielded a popular image of there being a fundamental psychological split in all humanity between the rational, analytic, linguistic, sequential Left Hemisphere and the visual, intuitive, divergent, synchronic Right Hemisphere. A vast variety of current ills have then been ascribed to an imbalanced dominance of the Left Hemisphere in western culture. Traditional polarities have become reformulated in hemispheric functioning terms: male (left) vs. female (right); scientific (left) vs. artistic (right); Western (left) vs. Eastern (right) cultural styles; even reason (left) vs. emotion (right). Much of this goes beyond anything the physiologists themselves are actually saying but the speed with which the physiological image of the split brain has been incorporated into popular psychology testifies to the sensitivity of PL to changes in physiological thinking. It is worth recalling that the term 'nervous breakdown' originated in the widely disseminated notion at the turn of the century of the hierarchical organization of the nervous system – mental illness being construed as a top-down collapse of this structure.

The history of Psychology can in principle be formulated in terms of a succession of physiomorphic moves of the kinds I have outlined here. These can take relatively simple forms such as Pribram's (1980) 'hologram theory of memory' – which at heart merely raises the possibility that the way a psychological function operates is analogous to the functioning of a novel piece of technology. They can also take more complex forms such as mathematical modelling and use of statistical techniques like factor analysis. Occasionally, as with Kelly's (1955) 'Personal Construct Theory', a psychologist aspires to some 'meta-psychological' position, but in Kelly's case only by adopting as the central image the notion that everyone is behaving like a scientist – again one wonders if this is really any different to earlier images of the self in terms of a professional role, as captain of a ship, as farmer, carpenter, king, or whatever.

CONCLUSION

In this chapter I have attempted to show how the physiomorphic perspective may be applied to the history of Psychology. It was argued that the discipline of Psychology evolved, in part at least, as an institutionalization of the physiomorphic process. Where, as in Watson's Behaviorism, Psychology has sought to sever itself from the normal PL generating process it has failed to make any long-term impact on PL. Where, as in Freud's case, it synthesizes a great many WL concepts its cultural impact can be substantial and the view of human nature embodied in the theory very difficult to supersede. The position adopted here clarifies the status of Psychology in an important way, by locating it within the physiomorphic process; Psychology is one route by which our changing knowledge of the world is mediated into changed conceptions of ourselves.

CHAPTER FIVE

PHYSIOMORPHISM IN HUMAN EVOLUTION

INTRODUCTION

That humans are unique is fairly self-evident. In what this uniqueness fundamentally consists is, by contrast, notoriously difficult to specify. Charles Darwin, in *The Descent of Man* (1871), effectively refuted many of the traditional candidates for the role: 'moral sense', curiosity, imagination, belief in God, intelligence, and the like. Since then, and especially over recent years, the difficulties of diagnosing what is uniquely human have continued to increase. The well-known ethological studies of primates and laboratory research on primate language capacities and self-consciousness have demonstrated that tool-use,[1] grief, rudimentary language skills, self-adornment, and reflexive self-awareness are present in our closest relatives. 'Culture' and language, of course, remain strong contenders, but the difficulty here is that neither of these can be thought of as suddenly appearing out of the blue. We are only forced back to the more basic question – what was it about humans which enabled them to evolve or acquire culture and modern language when no other primates effectively managed to?

The fact of the matter is that on current archaeological and palaeontological evidence a recognizably human species was in existence long before either culture or language were present in anything like their modern forms. During that long prelude, from the appearance of *Homo habilis* (slightly over two million years ago), via *Homo erectus* (from around 1.7 million years ago to less than half a million), to the first widely acknowledged, but isolated, evidence of 'art' (the Pêche de l'Aze rib) at 300,000 years,[2] a very slow, but nonetheless detectable, increase in human technological

103

skills occurs, while the species itself radiates from East Africa to the edges of the Eurasian landmass. The appearance of modern language and fully-fledged cultural life-styles is now generally placed at around 40,000 years ago, after the demise of the proto-cultural Neanderthals in Europe. 'Anatomically modern humans', on current evidence, date back around 100,000 years,[3] but what we might call 'Psychologically modern humans' less than half that time.

Already, prior to modern culture and language, the human behavioural repertoire had become more flexible and technologically sophisticated than anything elsewhere in the animal realm. Stone tools had changed from the crudely fashioned cobbles of the early Oldowan, associated with *H. habilis* (and possibly the australopithecine species *Paranthropus robustus*, see Susman 1988) to a highly elaborated kit of specialized tools requiring subtle and lengthy manufacturing procedures. Fire had been brought under control, certainly by 700,000, and some would argue more than 1,000,000, years ago. Shelters were made involving posts stuck in the ground; red ochre was being used (though what for is unknown); spears, digging sticks, and other wooden artefacts were in use; and the life-style was, in some places at least, structured around an annual cycle.[4] Culture and modern language thus appear to be as much of a culmination as a beginning in the evolution of humanity. To understand the psychological evolution of the species up to that point we need to identify what it was about the first hominids that uniquely set in train the cumulative processes of behavioural diversification, amplification of intelligence, and complexification of social structure, which made this culmination possible.

This topic is receiving increasing attention, and the prevalent approach now is to accept that processes at several different levels, from genetics to social structure, from diet to technology, were interacting. This can lead to mazes of feedback loops being postulated in which, for example, a change in diet might generate a change in technology which puts selective pressure on enhanced cognitive capacities in the brain which in turn enhance social skills, this affecting social structure which affects the nature of food-distribution which, to bring things full circle, changes the diet (see Blumenberg 1983, for example).

This kind of theorizing can certainly be valuable in facilitating the full articulation of all the variables in play, but it can divert us from the central issue too. What is it that we are trying, at heart, to explain? What is actually psychologically unique about humans? The answer is, I somewhat recklessly suggest, surprisingly simple. It is not anything specific that we do, like using language, or wearing clothes, or being creative; rather it is that we can do everything. Our behavioural repertoire is open-ended, both individually and, even more so, collectively. Taken individually any specific thing we do may be shown to be anticipated somewhere among our fellow animals. In the spirit of cutting the Gordian Knot, then, I propose that we take as the key question 'how can a species evolve an open-ended behavioural repertoire?' This is a psychological question which needs addressing if the operation of the other variables is to be correctly construed. And these other variables are significant insofar as they illuminate the necessary or sufficient conditions for behavioural amplification. The answer to this question, which the present chapter is concerned with elaborating, is that hominids evolved a new kind of learning strategy: physiomorphic learning.

PHYSIOMORPHIC LEARNING

Psychologists have recognized numerous types of learning, ranging from the genetically based 'imprinting' of many animal species, occuring in the early stages of life to enable the animal to identify its parent, to imitation and 'insight'. Many theorists believe that most of these, except the clearly genetically based ones, can be incorporated in a basic 'conditioning' framework. Kohler's 'insight learning' for example, which was held by Gestalt psychologists to refute the completeness of the conditioning account, was subsequently translated by Spence (e.g. 1938) into conditioning terms, while 'identification' was similarly treated by Gerwitz and Stingle (1968). Nevertheless, at the molar level, learning does present a variety of forms and it is with some caution that one advances yet another. Offsetting this is the fact that physiomorphic learning can be readily conceived as a generalized form of imitation, and thus in learning-theoretical terms does not propose anything new. Its novelty lies rather in the restructuring of the learning situation itself which its evolutionary emergence brought about.

The sequence of events involved in the evolution of physio-morphic learning,[5] a sequence which will enable us to define 'physiomorphism' somewhat more clearly than we have done so far, is relatively straightforward. Five stages may be postulated:

a) Primate imitation stage

As a primate we can reasonably assume that the earliest hominids shared the considerably developed imitative skills of their closest relatives, the chimpanzees. For our purposes we can think of imitation as a strategy for behavioural innovation which comes into play (like all other behavioural innovation strategies) when an existing, perhaps genetically 'wired in', problem-solving routine is blocked. We can also, rather crudely, view animal behaviour at this stage as comprising the sequential enactment of genetically-based life-routines. In the higher primates this sequential enactment is not rigidly constrained; nevertheless at any given point in time the animal is either in the process of enacting such a routine or is inactive. It is eating, searching for food, grooming, asserting its dominance or submission, engaged in some phase of mating behaviour, etc. Although temperamentally varied, chimpanzees have life-cycles, not biographies. They are living within the framework of a species-specific life-style, basically genetically determined (unless the *deus ex machina* of a Californian prima-tologist or *diabolos ex machina* of a medical vivisector intervenes). Within these constraints they may nevertheless initiate new forms of behaviour. The formal structure of imitation in these circumstances is to identify in the environment a procedure by which a particular life-routine-embedded goal may be achieved and copy it. This is more characteristic of juveniles than adults and is perhaps largely a spin-off from a more generalized phase of juvenile curiosity. The novel behaviours this yields nevertheless only persist insofar as they can be incorporated into species-specific life-routines. They may on occasion be established in a quasi-cultural way in the repertoire of a particular breeding group; after all it is the behaviour of other species members which is the primary environmental focus of imitative learning for the organism.

If we wish to model the structure of the internal storage of information at this stage we can see it as taking the form of a number of discrete amplifying loops at specific points in particular life-routine enactment programs. That is to say, an imitatively learned behaviour is initially associated/tagged/conditioned, to one point in the enactment of one life-routine. Only when the organism is at that point will the behaviour be exhibited. But if the same behaviour is required in the enactment of more than one life-routine the same imitatively learned substitute may well recur.

b) Proto-hominid imitation – initial amplification stage

Precisely why the pongid and hominid lines diverged has as yet eluded investigation. What we do know is that sometime around 6,000,000 years ago a small bipedal hominid (*Australopithecus afarensis*) was living in North East Africa. The precise reasons why bipedalism evolved are a matter for controversy, but it is clear that by then the ancestor was no longer living in the kind of environment now occupied by chimpanzees. The geological evidence suggests that the environment of this region at that time was highly variegated with mountains, rivers, forest, savannah, swamp, and sea represented within fairly close proximity to one another. Biologically this ancestor was perhaps slightly more capable of behavioural versatility than other primates but its brain was not appreciably bigger. For present purposes all we need to hypothesize is that this new, more variegated environment demanded a somewhat wider range of behavioural flexibility and presented a correspondingly wider range of environmental phenomena (the raw material for imitation) than did the more homogeneous forest environment. It is at least possible that there was some degree of aquatic involvement present, though this is not central to the present argument. Under these circumstances primate imitative capacities would be afforded greater scope and employed to a greater extent than hitherto. Such a situation would place increasing strain on the neurological information-storage capacities of the energetically expensive brain. Each life-routine program would have a large number of auxiliary amplifying loops and these would often be duplicated between such programs. At this stage, as with the previous one, the learned novel behaviour would also have to be fully represented internally. As the limits of this mode of information storage – behaviours directly and discretely linked to sequentially run life-routine programs – were approached, so the scene was set for a more efficient re-organization. This final phase in the elaboration of primate imitation abilities could well, one speculates, have corresponded to the emergence of *Homo habilis*.

c) Early hominid imitation – storage reversal

How could the storage of behavioural information be restructured? The two principle sources of difficulty we have noted are i) the unnecessary duplication of information relevant to more than one life-routine, and ii) the need for full representation of the behaviour. At this point it is useful to introduce a term for referring to the units of behaviour generated by imitation. Basically, in imitation, what is learned is that a certain behaviour X has an outcome Y, this sequence having been identified in the environment, X being within the organism's capacity to copy (or co-opt, e.g. in the case of using a stone tool the organism is co-opting the properties of broken stone into its own repertoire) and Y an outcome which furthers a life-routine. I will represent these as $X \rightarrow Y$ ('X causes Y'). The solution to the problem which I hypothesize here is that the structure of the storage was in a sense reversed. *Instead of $X \rightarrow Y$ units being tagged onto life-routines, the life-routines were tagged onto the $X \rightarrow Y$ units.*

This has two consequences: first, it means that a given $X \rightarrow Y$ need only be stored once; second, and more dramatically, it greatly reduces the need for full internal representation of X, since the environment itself can now serve this purpose. This second point will be clearer if we provide some hypothetical instances of the kind of change we envisage. A first example would be that at a certain stage in the butchery routine the individual reaches a 'break stone to crack bone' $X \rightarrow Y$ on finding the bone too hard for its teeth – it now sets about finding a suitable stone. To do this requires a full internal representation of the stone, the breaking of it, and so on to have been activated. After storage-reversal what happens is that on seeing an appropriate stone in its environment 'crack bone in butchery routine' is activated, the stone collected, and that stage in the butchery routine 'confirmed go' as one might say. Similarly, 'find gourd to carry the water' reverses to 'keep for carrying water' on finding an appropriate gourd; 'collect big leaves for shelter' reverses to 'collect for shelter' on coming across suitable leaves, and so on. Instead of full representation all that is required is recognition.

I have detailed some of the more complex consequences of this situation and how it could have arisen elsewhere (Richards 1989), notably the effects it has on the way in which life-routines are themselves enacted, becoming both more fragmented and more intertwined. This constitutes an initial 'time-binding' exercise as it involves a greater integration of future and past needs and behaviours. Carrying technology may well have been a very significant move here since it represents a kind of generalized notion of future needs – what is to be carried may vary but that something will need to be carried is now incorporated into the overall life-style.

This new situation facilitates a much greater flexibility of group behaviour than before, and it releases the neurological resources for further, more efficient, incorporation into the behavioural repertoire of environmentally identified X→Ys. Yet it still constrains behaviour ultimately within the life-routines. For a number of reasons I believe this stage probably lasted for the duration of the *Homo erectus* period.

The record of the behaviour of *Homo erectus* is enigmatic in a number of respects. Technological advance was very slow, but their tool-making skills were considerable, and, although they spread throughout the Eurasian landmass, they do not appear to have engaged in any distinctively 'cultural' behaviour – variation in stone tools being accountable for by differences in raw materials. Their brain-size was approaching that of modern *Homo sapiens* but the actual rate of behavioural innovation seems strangely lethargic. They still, we might say, seem to have had life-cycles rather than biographies. If the present account is correct this is what we would expect. On the one hand it accounts for the capacity for behavioural innovation and environmental adaptation which facilitated their radiation, but on the other hand depicts them as living lives organized exclusively around the genetically-determined primate life-routines, albeit now enacted in more complex ways.

d) Generalized imitation – 'physiomorphism'

At this point a further method of simplifying the transactions between an organism and its environment can emerge. Although in principle Stage 3 might have continued indefinitely, it is ultimately precarious in its foundations. As the ratio of genetically-wired-in behaviour to imitatively-based behaviour gets smaller, as the actual enactment of life-routines becomes more flexible and complex, the role of the original, fully-elaborated, 'wired-in' life-routine becomes less and less important. What was originally the central point of reference for all behaviour, from which X→Ys were but short detours, becomes increasingly redundant. What remains significant is the motivational basis for the life-routines. All we need to know is that we are hungry; how we act on that depends on the precise situation we see ourselves as being in, which will determine exactly what combination of X→Y units in our repertoire are appropriate. We might, after all, only need to go to the nut-store, (having long ago learned that from the squirrels?).

The logical next step then is to abandon life-routine tagging altogether. The whole problem can be solved by the neat and economic step of living according to the general rule 'For any Y identify an X and copy'. Under these circumstances the exploration of the X→Y possibilities in the environment acquires an imperative of its own. They are no longer interesting only insofar as they can be immediately related to a particular life-routine but because *any* X→Y might prove valuable for some purpose or other at some time in the future. The advantages to the individual, and *inter alia*, to the group, of maximizing their repertoire of such 'knowledge' would soon have become apparent.

Physiomorphism then first appears in the form of the generalized learning program 'For any Y identify X and copy'. But how do you copy? Copying involves, essentially, being like the X in our X→Y unit. The primary epistemological tactic, therefore, could also be expressed 'To know something, become like it'. And how you might become like something can take many forms, including wearing its skin and eating it as well as overt behavioural copying (which would include making noises like it).

Nonetheless, refuge in physiomorphic learning, like every other form of refuge, has its price. What has happened here is nothing less than the abandonment of a species-specific behavioural identity. The 'wired-in' life-routines provide a species with its underlying behavioural coherence just as much as the other genetic factors ensure its bio-morphological coherence. Abandon them and the species faces the possibility of what might be termed 'behavioural evaporation'. It is precisely at this point that our model sheds light on the contentious issue of the origin of culture. If a behavioural species-identity has gone, it has to be replaced by another method of ensuring the integrity of the group. This can only be achieved by instituting some collective evaluation of the vast number of behaviours now within the group's repertoire. Furthermore, whatever physiomorphic identifications an individual has in its personal repertoire, its core identity has to be with the group as such. Culture then begins as a way of ensuring the continued behavioural coherence of the group, providing its members with an identity separate from any of those offered (some very seductively) by the natural world around them. This 'Culture/Nature' distinction is of course familiar to anthropologists. Differences *between* human cultures perhaps necessarily ensue in due course, but the primary move is the differentiation of the human group from nature itself. Many advantages accrue, both individually and collectively, under these circumstances. Collectively the group will have at its disposal a greatly enhanced range of responses (instead of a single typical species-specific one) to problem situations corresponding to the individual skills of its members. Individually, the onus is no longer on managing to successfully enact a set of genetically determined behavioural routines, but on creating a socially useful role for oneself on the basis of whatever genetic legacy one has received. This implies, it should be stressed, a dramatic shift in the focus of natural selection processes. For the first time even the blind now have an above zero likelihood of surviving, while morphological variations can be exploited in the acquisition of behavioural skills particularly suitable for them; the small wiry individual can be as useful as the big strong muscular one.

It seems reasonable to suggest that the early phases of Stage 4 began to occur in the immediate post-*Homo erectus* phase with what are at present called 'Archaic *Homo sapiens*', a term covering a number of fossils from the period around 500,000 years to 100,000 years ago (although some from Omo in Ethiopia dated at 1,000,000 years old are classified here too). These generally possessed larger brains than *H. erectus*, as well as being more anatomically similar to modern humans in other respects. For the first time we find traces of apparently non-functional decoration (the Pêche de l'Aze rib mentioned earlier) and an increased tempo in the rate of stone tool development, as well as a dramatic expansion in the tool-kit size. Non-functional regional variations in style of stone tool manufacture can also be identified. The most advanced Stage 4 *Homo sapiens* species was probably the Neanderthals (not now thought to be directly ancestral to us) whose 'Mousterian' style of tool manufacture reached very sophisticated levels and who, on archaeological evidence, appear to have cared for their sick and elderly (anybody above forty probably!), and buried their dead (in at least one known case, Shanidar in Iran, with flowers).

In spite of a behavioural level verging on the modern there is nonetheless something still missing from the apparent behaviour of our ancestors and Neanderthal close relatives prior to 40,000 years or so ago. Even allowing for the ravages of time the sudden absence of much that can be called 'artistic' prior to that point is remarkable. Sophisticated as they are by comparison with the preceding period, their stone tools remain rather crude and robust by comparison with those made subsequently. And the demise of the physically robust and very large-brained Neanderthals in Europe has to be accounted for. Current opinion among those studying human prehistory and evolution is beginning to coalesce around the notion that the key factor separating the pre-modern proto-cultural from the fully modern phase is indeed the appearance of fully developed, syntactically structured, and lexically encoded language. This is not to say that vocal channel communication had not reached a high level of development prior to this; indeed we must assume it had. This then marks the fifth of the stages in human psychological evolution being identified here.

e) Linguistic encoding

The most far-reaching consequence of Stage 4, as we have just seen, was the emergence of a need for collective evaluation of the vast number of items now in the behavioural repertoire. In itself this need not entail a fully developed language of the modern type; a relatively restricted vocabulary of signals would suffice to encode basic good/bad distinctions, while transmission of behavioural skills can be effectively managed by copying together with a small number of signals carrying such meanings as 'no', 'yes', 'good', 'harder', 'careful', and the like, which can readily be achieved by non-grammatical, and only rudimentarily lexical, morphemes. Many theorists argue that it was in the realm of social relations rather than technology that the pressures for linguistic evolution were most intense, and social relations would also have become increasingly complex as the behavioural repertoire expanded. Even so, a communication system based on non-grammatical vocal signalling and gesture (including facial expression) can suffice for a long time.

Early theorists on the origin of language sought the answer in a number of relatively simple processes such as imitation of animal sounds or noises made by struck objects, expressive exclamations, and vocal play.[6] Although nobody now accepts these as constituting the whole story, it remains reasonable to assume that an expansion of the noise-making repertoire would have occurred as a result of the physiomorphic process, and that, whatever their original source, noises could have begun to acquire increasingly differentiated signal-properties. Yet however elaborate the repertoire of vocal channel signals became it could not generate modern language in any simple fashion, two key features of which are a) that the relationship between morpheme and referent is arbitrary and b) syntactic structuring of utterances. The precise manner in which modern language evolved from its immediate precursor is as yet unknown, but it almost certainly involved physiological changes in the laryngeal system (Leiberman 1984) as well as psychological processes. Further speculation on how this momentous move was achieved will serve no purpose here. What we can argue, though, is that the situation initiated by Stage 4 possesses a far higher dynamic for change than those preceding it. Once the rate of growth of the behavioural repertoire is enhanced, the social, proto-cultural, structures required for its evaluation and integration will have to change at a similar pace. Cross-generational transmission of information, 'education' regarding the group's values, and so forth will have to take progressively more elaborate forms.

Once again the existing psychological and social mechanisms for storing information will come under pressure as the consequences of entering a new Stage accumulate. The individual is now having to respond to environmental phenomena with a far greater degree of discrimination than before, and for the first time the collective evaluation (or social meaning) of phenomena has to be psychologically represented as a further kind of knowledge. But, behind all this, the individual is also having to create and maintain a social identity for itself within the group, one based on its personally-acquired behavioural repertoire rather than on genetically-based species-specific age and sex roles. (Not that the latter disappear, of course; however they are no longer sufficient in themselves.) It is within the context of this mounting pressure, and I believe in response to it, that modern language emerges. A very important consequence of this should be immediately noted: the location of information storage is again changed. In Stages 1 and 2 we saw that information was stored exclusively within the organism; in Stages 3 and 4 this was supplemented, and the functional role of internal storage radically changed, by the advent of environmental storage. In this final stage a third level is added: the cultural. The functional roles of the other two levels are again modified in consequence.

At this point we have nearly come full circle in our exposition. In Chapter 2 we saw how the very existence of language entailed the identification of the self as a speaker. In the latter phases of Stage 4 the imperative to develop a social identity over and above the biological was, it has been argued above, intensifying as a consequence of the need for collective evaluation of behaviour if group coherence was to be sustained. Such collective evaluation will be mediated primarily by linguistic means, even though these means have not yet acquired the specificity and refinement which modern language affords. The identification of self as speaker will thus have its origins in the immediately pre-modern language phase. With the advent of modern language the identification of self as speaker can finally triumph over all other identifications as the core of self-hood; but as the language is an external, collective product such an identification will embed the individual firmly within the group. Having an identity as a speaker of the group's language will both inhibit anti- and non-group identifications and at the same time allow access to the collective, linguistically encoded repertoire of identifications.

Furthermore, the advent of modern language, with its discrete lexical naming and syntactic resources, will facilitate an even more rapid extension of physiomorphic identifications while ensuring that the extension is under collective control. Individual personhood can be fully articulated in terms of the PL which this now-labelled and categorized corpus of identifications affords. There is no place within this account for the view, once almost traditional among speculators on the 'primitive' condition, that there was a period when 'inner' and 'outer' were not differentiated. What has varied is where the boundary lines between the two are to be drawn, particularly in the case of anomalous phenomena such as dream experiences. And here we have returned to the vicissitudes of referential mode preference discussed in Chapter 2.

A final advantage of modern language, discussed by Lieberman (1984), is the sheer rapidity of information exchange which it renders possible. This, as Lieberman indicates, is not simply a matter of speed but of complexity. This had previously been restricted by the limits of the short-term memory span, and while this time-span as such might not have increased, a far greater number of operations could be completed within it. He in fact diagnoses the downfall of the Neanderthals as due to precisely this fact: their rival *Homo sapiens sapiens* could simply collectively outwit them by the superiority of modern language over the more ponderous communication system of the Neanderthals.

Stage 5 therefore represents the culmination of the evolution of physiomorphic learning. Language itself may still be reasonably seen as having its ultimate roots in the physiomorphic assimilation of animals' noises etc. which the nineteenth century linguists loved to invoke, but these would have been insufficient to generate modern language. The precise mechanism whereby lexical syntactic modern language finally emerged out of the complex matrix of factors in play during Stage 4 remains undiagnosed. Writers such as Holloway (1981), Fox (1979), Hewes (1973) and Jaynes (1976) have drawn attention to a whole host of ways in which the elaboration of vocal communication would have been reinforced, and they will not be further rehearsed here. What ought to be noted, though, is that modern language fuses both the social and informational functions of communication. It is fundamentally a 'laminated' phenomenon in which layers with differing evolutionary depth have become integrated. Pre-lexical, emotional-signal, expressive intonation underlies grammatical structure while onomatopoeic imitative elements no doubt underpinned, however obscurely, at least some of the elaboration of lexical features. The notion that even grammar and arbitrary naming appeared in a single move is probably an over-simplification, although once their rudiments had appeared their subsequent maturation was undoubtedly rapid. All I wish to insist on in the present account is that modern language emerged as a solution to the pressures on social organization and social life which physiomorphic learning created. And in solving them it opened up the way to an even more efficient operation of physiomorphism, creating a situation in which the dynamic of events was further accelerated.

This process has received two further boosts. The first is the invention of writing which places information storage back into the physical world, rather than in the collective verbal memory. This heightens the rate of cross-generational accumulation of information, as well as bringing about long-term psychological changes which we need not explore here (such as altering time-perspective and changing the social function of memory). The second was the invention of printing. These are each reminiscent in their way of Stage 3 – in Stage 3 the natural world became a sort of library of possible behaviours for the individual to draw on. Now the library is itself created, the individual only needs to store knowledge about where information is held. A third boost is perhaps the advent of electronic media. But we are now into Marshall McLuhan (1964) country!

To summarize this section: it is proposed that five stages may be identified by which primate imitative learning became transformed into linguistically-mediated physiomorphic learning. The primate condition became strained as a result of the build-up of discrete X→Y units, a build-up due to the changed conditions of early hominid life in a variegated environment demanding heightened behavioural flexibility. This was resolved by a transformation of the storage structure, in which life-routine enactment was organised around the X→Y units themselves. Information was now stored in the environment itself. As the repertoire of X→Y units increased, so the role of the genetically-built-in life-routines diminished and a further simplifying move became possible: adoption of the generalized physiomorphic program 'to achieve Y identify an X and copy', which can also be expressed 'to know what something is, be like it'. In time this creates a major problem for maintenance of social coherence since behaviour is no longer constrained within species-specific confines. This can only be solved by mechanisms for collective evaluation of behaviour, a move wherein the origins of 'culture' can be identified. Finally, the mounting complexities of social life, as the behavioural repertoire continues to increase, give rise to a situation in which an already well-developed vocal communication system is transformed into modern language. This remedies earlier difficulties by anchoring individuals firmly within their language community; at the same time it enhances physiomorphic learning to an even greater degree by the refinements in discrimination and information exchange which accompany it.

PHYSIOMORPHIC BEHAVIOUR: I

Physiomorphism is not then a purely linguistic matter. As has been stated several times the process can be mediated by behavioural imitation, dance, dress, ornamentation, and consumption. One implication of the argument of the previous section is that we can view the human past as a succession of identifications, an accumulation of incorporations into the human repertoire of the phenomena, properties, and processes of the natural world. In the light of this we need to re-read the significance of a great deal of material which has hitherto been too readily subsumed into frameworks which take primitive anthropomorphism as axiomatic. But before doing so it will be useful to consider in more detail precisely what it is about us that enables us to engage in physiomorphic behaviour.

The hominid body, via evolutionary processes still not completely unravelled, acquired a number of features which jointly amounted to rendering it a 'universal tool' for behavioural modelling. Much emphasis is placed on our bipedalism, but the significance of this lies partly in the fact that an upright posture constitutes one end of a wide postural continuum. Coupled as it is with a fine sense of balance our bipedalism also enabled us to adopt a vast variety of other postures: one-legged balancing, stooping, crouching, sitting, leaning, and craning, etc., non-bipedal locomotive modes such as crawling, knee-and-hand quadrupedalism, swimming, climbing, brachiating, even rolling and sliding downhill on one's bottom are all in our repertoire. Whatever changes occurred in hominid morphological evolution, previous gains were apparently rarely sacrificed. The additional advantages of prehensile hands are too obvious and numerous to require listing here. Hairlessness was also important because it enabled us to modify our appearance by clothing, pigmentation, and decoration, although this was not why it evolved in the first place. The net effect of this 'universal tool' morphology was, in short, to enable us to continually modify our appearance and behaviour, incorporating temporarily into our physiology a vast number of 'attachments' from belts to hats, spears to masks, earrings to spectacles, shoes to gloves, and armour to amulets. Leonard Williams (1980) has also argued that humans are unlike other primates in possessing a sense of rhythm. This rhythmic sense is possibly a consequence of bipedal walking and cortical lateralization of function. Whatever its origins, it too serves as a basis for modelling rhythmic natural phenomena, and nowhere more so than in dancing (see Chapter 3). The disappearance of species-specific identity discussed earlier in behavioural terms is thus reflected in our morphology itself, which lends itself to an endless variety of metamorphoses. And to each of these variations in posture, appearance, and behaviour corresponds a psychological state. Nevertheless, the raw material for these transformations comes from outside; it is that external world which is being cumulatively incorporated, until our transactions with it consist of a perpetual juggling with its own, not our 'wired-in', properties. We continually set its properties against one another for our anthropocentric, not anthropomorphic, ends.

The reality of physiomorphism as a psychological process must be insisted upon here, although its full intensity is often obscured for us today. One of its most dramatic forms is so-called 'possession' in which a particular animal identification takes over the individual completely (e.g. the 'leopard men' cults of West Africa), and indeed the potency of animal identifications is testified at many levels. The 'beast within' image beloved of the later Victorians, the idea that within each of us lurks a primitive bestial savage nature is one expression of this; it is not after all a dark and hidden side of *human* nature but a persisting awareness of the vulnerability of what I above termed the 'social self' to *non*-human identifications of an overpowering kind (the 'werewolf' theme being another example). Much of human cultural history, particularly the history of religious and mythological beliefs, can be re-read as a record of the efforts of culture to map, master, and control such identifications. Although it is beyond the scope of the present work to deal with religion and mythology in any detail something does need to be said about these matters.

RELIGION AND MYTHOLOGY

Mythology, Joseph Campbell (1984) tells us, serves four functions; in pride of place he puts the mystical function: '...to awaken and maintain in the individual a sense of wonder and participation in the mystery of this finally inscrutable universe'; second, '...to fill every particle and quarter of the current cosmological image with its measure of this mystical import'; third, the sociological function of '...validating and maintaining whatever moral system and manner of life-customs may be peculiar to the local culture'; and finally '...the pedagogical [function]...of conducting individuals in harmony through passages of human life' (1984:8-9). It is with no little trepidation that one ventures to oppose an authority with such an encyclopaedic knowledge of mythology as Campbell, but our model leaves us little choice. I have no quarrel with the final two functions, but the first two appear highly suspect, at least in the terms in which Campbell couches them. In this section I will outline an alternative programmatic sketch of how mythologies evolved in the light of the physiomorphic model. This is highly tentative but may serve to demystify the subject.

i) The situation we have been describing is one in which the group is faced with an ongoing task of holding socially disruptive identifications at bay, without inhibiting their exploration. In order to achieve this there must be a mechanism which ensures that the core identification of individual members is with the group. Language, we saw, plays a crucial role in this. The situation is, even so, far from secure. While naming is a step towards mastery it is far from sufficient. The natural environment with which the group is in constant interaction contains numerous phenomena which have as yet been unassimilated, or only partially so. In the earlier phases this would probably include various animals, intoxicating plants, the weather, seasonal changes, the Sun and Moon, and perhaps even geological phenomena such as volcanoes. Also, as the weight of physiomorphic identifications accumulates so the counterweight of mechanisms for maintaining primary identification with the group has to be increased.

ii) In this context a number of procedures may be adopted. First, a procedure by which physiomorphic flooding ('possession') can be brought under control by creating certain occasions on which it is sanctioned, occasions carefully structured to ensure its containment. Second, a procedure which guarantees that all individual members of the group have direct experience of the most potent identifications within the cultural repertoire, thereby also learning how to control such identifications, and acquiring an understanding of the basis for their received collective evaluation. Third, the collective evaluation itself will take the form of an attempted full assimilation of the 'best' identifications as content for the group's own 'cultural' self-identification, i.e. a full 'humanization' of the property in question so that it becomes part of the 'counterweight' just mentioned. Fourth, the provision of an institutionalized mapping and structuring of the framework of identifications within terms of which human life within the group is conducted.

iii) The function of these procedures, within which we can readily recognize such phenomena as initiation rites, ritual dance, shamanism, 'spirit possession' states, 'totemism', sacrifice, and mythical cosmologies, is thus the very reverse of what has customarily been thought and taught. Far from constituting anthropomorphic projections, attempts at participating in cosmic life and generally infusing the world with mystery, they are techniques for holding the cosmos at bay, for channelling and controlling participation in the cosmic life so that both individual and group identities are preserved. The goal is to tame and domesticate the natural powers, and precisely *not* to overwhelmingly identify with them. Identifications have to be constantly constrained and managed, for they can be very dangerous. It hardly needs saying that the pervasive facts of birth, sex, and death which ultimately continue to bind humans into the processes of nature will serve as constant thematic foci for these procedures.

iv) In time the recursive operation of these procedures and

continued extension of the behavioural repertoire will yield cultural products of a familiar form: animal headed deities, ritual placations and negotiations with natural powers, and more sophisticated cosmological myths. It must, though, be kept in mind that, as was explained in Chapter 2, the ascription of personhood to an agency is not the same as the ascription of humanity, for at heart personhood and 'language user' or 'speaker/listener' are synonymous and there is always a fundamental ambiguity as to whether an agency is a non-language user or merely using a language of which one is ignorant.

v) Our current, or recently current, neat differentiations between animacy and inanimacy, between the different ways in which things come into being, between what is 'human' and what is non-human, between reason and unreason, and indeed between Mind and Matter, have all been differentiated *out of* earlier frameworks for construing the world and our experience. There is no clear sense in which these earlier phases were *mistaken* and we are *right*.[7]

At this juncture a number of possible misunderstandings of the position being adopted here should be answered. First, I am not denying that people do use mythological and religious frameworks as routes towards experiences of the kind Campbell referred to. What I would hold is that such uses and aspirations can only occur after the core identifications of the group are secure and in the light of a fully developed cosmology in which nature *is* depicted as harmonious, orderly, and ultimately benevolent. As to which comes first, the 'mystical experience' or the cosmology, this is very much a chicken and egg question. What concerns me here is that it is highly *un*likely that Nature presented itself in these terms in the first place; the task of the human group was initially to maintain an identity for itself over and above the natural world (which was at once seductive and threatening, nurturing and dangerous) while remaining physiomorphically engaged with it. In an important sense however the quest for mystical union in its more developed forms (e.g. in Buddhism) represents a counter-move to physiomorphic identification, a procedure by which identifications can either be stripped away or a single all-sufficient identification achieved. The fairly common twentieth-century Psychological account of this as rooted in a wish for 'regression to the womb' is inadequate. Clearly procedures for eliminating identifications will eventually come to have an important place in contexts where the repertoire has become especially luxuriant; at least somewhere in the culture there must be a representation of the insight that these *are* but identifications and the products ultimately of the operations of consciousness *per se.*

Second, I am not proposing any Comtean evolutionary structure of the way human thought has developed. There is no necessary inner logic taking us through religion to philosophy and thence to science. The actual forms which cosmological thought, religious, philosophical, or 'scientific', takes in different cultures will be determined by a whole range of factors, from the physical environment to specific historical experiences and the idiosyncratic influence of single powerful individuals. Some of these forms may be highly stable for millenia, as in the case of the Upper Palaeolithic, Egyptian, Chinese, and native Australian cultures. Globally considered the last ten millenia at least do nonetheless present a picture of cumulative and accelerating physiomorphic mastery of 'Nature' which appears to be in some current state of culmination.

Third, I am not trying to claim that the physiomorphic account offered here constitutes an explanation of all and everything pertaining to religious and mythological thought. Certainly, in the case of creation myths particularly, a number of different levels of psychological concern seem to be involved, notably the origins of the external world, the origins of consciousness as such, and the origins of individual consciousness. My suspicion here is that there may well be crisis points in the collective elaboration and management of physiomorphic identifications (analogous, but only analogous, to those precipitating the stage-shifts in the Piagetian account of cognitive development) in which the inner/outer distinction *is* temporarily suspended and everything goes, as it were, into the melting pot, a mythology emerging from this as a quasi-Kuhnian paradigm, a cosmological account within which thought over the subsequent 'normal' phase can be conducted. The sheer ambiguity, multivalence and polyfunctional character of mythologies is, even so, of their very essence; they are the nearest thing to utterances which are truly neutral regarding referential mode, and serve both to define and override the inner/outer boundary.

It is appropriate here to note that advanced religious belief systems have provided quite a number of PL terms such as: *pious, blasphemous, karma, reverent, holy, blessed,* and the like. Even so, they were not created *ab novo* in these religious senses: *pious* originally meant *dutiful; holy* comes from an inferred Germanic term *hailaz* = whole; *blessed* from an inferred Germanic term *blodham* = mark with blood; and so on.

Finally, what has been said in this section is intended to serve only as a preliminary indication of ways in which religious, mythological, and cosmological thought (between which it is difficult to rigorously discriminate) may be construed from the physiomorphic perspective. It is thus, at best, programmatic in character, seeking only to place certain questions on the agenda.

PHYSIOMORPHIC BEHAVIOUR: II

The range of behaviours which might be considered as mediating the physiomorphic process has been noted in passing several times and received some attention in Chapter 3. These will now be considered somewhat more extensively.

a) Overt behavioural imitation

James Fernandez (1974),[8] in a paper which anticipated in part the present thesis (although not recognizing the problematic nature of the concept 'metaphor' itself), wrote:

Is it not arguable that primordially animals are predicates by which subjects obtain an identity and are thus objects of affinity and participation? If so, the first problem is not how animals take human shape, but how humans take animal shape and enact nature. In fact there is plentiful evidence that animals have been such primordial *points de repère* in the pronouns' (the essential inchoate subjects') quest for identity.
(1974:121)

He goes on to cite numerous children's games in which animal roles are explored, wolves, leopards, horses, donkeys, and sheep figuring prominently. He also notes 'An acquaintance was very disturbed by his two-year-old's habit of climbing up on the back of a sofa or the piano and leaping off like the family cat' (1974:122). I recall a television interview with the actor Peter Ustinov in which he confessed that at one time during his early childhood he became a car and spent his time brrrm brrrrm-ing around the house. Most families could probably provide similar anecdotes of infantile physiomorphic behavioural identification. This capacity is, as was discussed above, facilitated by the 'universal tool' character of human morphology. The highest form this has taken may be found in the yoga asanas, of which, according to one authority, there are no fewer than 8,400,000! 'The postures are as many in number as there are living creatures in the universe' (Hewitt 1960, quoting Gheranda Samhita). Since some postures are named after artefacts (e.g. the bow and the plough), perhaps the number should be even higher. The injuction 'to understand something, be like it' is, in yoga, quite straightforwardly implemented; the individual directly attempts to model the characteristic posture of an animal and meditates on what it is to be in this form. While yoga is essentially passive, more obviously practical methods of modelling animal behaviour occur in the children's games mentioned earlier – in which important prey and predator identities are mastered – and above all in dance (discussed in Chapter 3). While overt behavioural modelling is the paradigm example of physiomorphic behaviour the boundary-line with other forms is blurred.

b) Clothing and adornment

The effects on one's behaviour of wearing fancy dress are familiar to most of us. Don a cowboy hat and drawling and swaggering immediately ensue; a British policeman's helmet by contrast yields a rocking, legs apart, stance with hands clasped behind the back; while dressing in the clothes of the opposite sex can have far more dramatic effects. While these effects are in part merely an adoption of culturally stereotyped roles, this only pushes the problem back one stage further – why did *these* forms of dress come to be adopted by those taking these roles in the first place? The connection between costume and social role is not arbitrary; it was not mere whim that led Nazis to choose tight-fitting uniforms with copious use of black leather accessories rather than frilly shirts and tweed trousers as their hallmark. Costume is obviously functionally related to the role being required of the wearer; but what is striking is the immediacy of the integration of functional and stylistic components into an overall identity-gestalt. Historically, changes in fashion cannot be differentiated from cultural change as a whole, and the typical costumes of a particular period or region carry with them direct psychological connotations regarding the attitude to life, beliefs, behavioural style, and even temperament of the wearer. Togas go with classical columns, declamatory oratory and self-importance; the Elizabethan costume with half-timbered houses, patriotism, and a general theatrical manner. Again, stereotypes, but again the question arises as to how dress acquires such immediate, specific, and complex signal values. Given that this *is* in fact the case, that the mere wearing of a particular kind of hat can wreak serious changes in one's self-image (at least temporarily), what of wrapping oneself in an entire animal skin?

Physiomorphism can be mediated therefore by incorporation of the object in question into one's morphology by affixing it to one's body. From precious stones to feathers, from bones to whole animal skins, from flowers to metals, the human race has continually worn the natural world. We drape it over us, we stick it through our noses, ears, and lips, we tie it onto us, we hang it on our limbs, and we daub it on our skin and in our hair. In doing this we are assimilating to ourselves, for all kinds of purpose, the properties of the materials in which we are thus clad and garlanded. If a stone fascinates me, I will become fascinating to others by wearing it. But it is not quite this simple. Wearing something does not always of itself constitute the physiomorphic move, but rather signals or symbolizes the identifications of the wearer. To wear a snake or a leopard skin signals that the wearer has mastered and assimilated the snake or leopard identity, probably by killing it. Prior to modern weaponry the killing of an animal entailed knowing enough about it to outwit it; to kill the snake meant first identifying with the snake in order to understand it; killing it signalled both that one had identified with it *and* that one had mastered the identification. The shaman's miscellaneous clutter of accessories is visible evidence of the number of identifications which he has under his belt. The situation becomes more complex when the power of the identification comes to be metonymically invested in the symbol as such, the power of the bear *is* in its claws for example, so wearing the bear claw is in itself sufficient to acquire the appropriate identification, as was wearing the policeman's helmet. Such a move is often labelled as illogical, magical thinking. This, though, is to side-step the issue. Psychologically we do, as a matter of fact, experience the power of an identification as pervading 'symbols' of this kind. True, we may need to be part of the culture in order to experience this; we have to already know the symbol's 'meaning'. Placing a bishop's mitre on one's head would amount to little more than putting on a funny hat if one had no knowledge of the Christian Church. But it is a peculiar argument to claim that the immunity of the ignorant outsider is somehow 'truer' than the susceptibility of the knowing insider, that 'really' it *is* only a funny hat.

I believe psychologists as yet understand relatively little about the mechanisms which render cultural artefacts at all levels so phenomenologically coherent – what it is, say, that unifies Victorian costume, jewellery, furniture, novels, paintings, typefaces, music, architecture, porcelain, stamps, book-bindings, science, political policies, and even crimes so that they all seem to share some common aura. What is referred to as a period 'atmosphere' or *Zeitgeist*, infusing all the products of the time, does, though, link up ultimately with the process whereby the wearing of an eagle's claw endows the wearer, both for him- or herself and for others in their group, with some eagle-like property. The process rendering such a person aquiline is surely at some level the same as that which renders a wearer of a top hat and tail-coat a Victorian. If we are right in seeking the answer in this direction then physiomorphism is a far more imponderably fluid, 'stickier', or 'contagious' process than we might originally have suspected.

c) Eating and drinking

Even more literally than behavioural modelling, eating or drinking something incorporates it into oneself. This does not, though, extend to all dietary items, or rather their 'meaning' as food is sufficient; one does not become chicken-like simply by eating a chicken, and water is usually just water in this context.[9] On the other hand food is one of the most culturally elaborated areas of social life. Dietary rules regarding what can be eaten, when it

126

can be eaten, how it is to be prepared, and who is to eat it have fascinated anthropologists over the last fifty years or so, and what is to be said here is in a sense only a footnote to the labours of Lévi-Strauss, Mary Douglas, Edmund Leach *et al.*

One topic very relevant to us is the consumption of intoxicants. For any group living in an environment where intoxicant plants and fungi are available a cultural codification and construal of their effects will be a matter of some importance, even perhaps urgency if they are in any sense addictive or the effects are especially pleasurable. The dramatic alterations in psychological state engendered by intoxicants consitute 'possession' of a most clear-cut kind, only initially explicable in terms of a direct access to the various essential 'natures' of the plants or fungi which provide their source. And unlike the case in behavioural imitation this 'nature' is psychological rather than behavioural in kind. It is a direct *psychological* encounter effectively 'proving' that the psychological is not restricted to humans alone. Furthermore, via the alterations in perception by which it is constituted, this non-human psychological condition in which the human is now participating grants access to aspects of the world normally closed off – or perhaps to a different world altogether? While within this state of possession then the individual *may also engage in physiomorphic transactions of other kinds with the phenomena thus revealed.* A comprehensive cosmology will now have to incorporate the cosmos as revealed during intoxication, and an understanding of that cosmology will involve experiencing it.[10] The intoxicant becomes an agent of knowledge. Contemporary taboos on the whole topic of intoxicants, other than alcohol, may be seriously hampering a full appreciation of their significance as a factor in our psychological and cultural evolution. It is possible of course for anthropologists to investigate Latin American peyote cults in depth, but the roles of cannabis, amanita, ergot, and opium in Western religious and cultural history have rarely been fully confronted, and when they have, as in Allegro (1973), contumely has generally fallen on the author's head.

At a less extreme, but more patently practical, level the physiomorphic exploration of plant properties by direct consumption resulted in the discovery of a range of herbal therapeutic agents and, their opposite, toxins.

Unlike the other kinds of physiomorphic identification we have been discussing, identification by ingestion is temporary, lasting only as long as the substance is pharmacologically active in the body. In order to retain the 'knowledge' thus obtained, resort must be made to procedures for transferring it from the intoxicated state to normal consciousness. This is achieved primarily by such means as painting or carving representations of the world as seen under intoxication, or composing songs, poems, and stories about it. In this way the experience also becomes amenable to social control and structuring, these cultural products providing maps for, and pre-structuring the expectations of, those subsequently using the intoxicant.

The concept of physiomorphism thus seems to provide a route for linking a variety of typically human behaviours. It could perhaps be extended even further to include, as the final comment implies, much artistic behaviour. As cultural complexity and the weight of the historical legacy a culture carries increase, so the original character of the underlying physiomorphic dynamic becomes obscured; genuinely anthropomorphic reprojections of by now human qualities onto phenomena other than their original sources will occur; distortions and mystifications will enter into the record of past physiomorphic experience as that record is continually restructured to legitimate the present structure of socio-economic relations; while simple misunderstanding and accidental loss will make their own confusing contributions. To most of us today the very nature of mythological systems has become elusive; what, we puzzle, were the Norse myths really *about?* We can read them as stories, submit them to psychodynamic interpretation, attempt euhemeristic decoding, or view them as synchronic thought-structures in Lévi-Straussian fashion, but since we are not *living* within the reality they defined, they have ceased, to use a Jungian term, to be numinous. Bury oneself in Frazer's *The Golden Bough*, the collected works of Jung, Lévi-Strauss or Mircea Eliade for a year or two and one may feel illumination dawning, but is what one is understanding the original myth or a meta-myth created by one's chosen savant? Few anthropologists now place much weight on the accounts of 'primitive mentality' by such writers as Lévy Bruhl, Frazer, and Durkheim which appeared in the earlier years of the present century, yet their contemporaries were positively inspired by them, feeling they provided a genuine reconnection to ancestral roots. Our account leaves these higher cultural products relatively untouched, but does offer the suggestion that we may be able to discern within them a record of physiomorphic identifications and the struggles to keep them under control.

As our earlier discussions of PL and Psychological theorizing indicated, the physiomorphic process still continues, and its behavioural as well as linguistic forms are also still with us if we know how to look. After all, what else is the wearer of a Sony Walkman doing?

THE EVOLUTION OF INTELLIGENCE

This final section is by way of a clarification of the way in which the present account relates to the approaches of Parker and Gibson (1979) and Thomas Wynn (1979; 1981). These have both offered models of hominid psychological evolution which utilize a broadly Piagetian approach, viewing the process as involving the acquisition of cognitive operations of progressively greater complexity formally defineable in Piagetian terms. The evidence for this development can be found both in artefacts (e.g. in the progression from Oldowan choppers to Acheulean hand-axes exhibiting symmetry in all three dimensions) and in what can be inferred of hominid life-styles at various points, either from archaeological evidence or, more tenuously, from morphology. Parker and Gibson seek to tie these developments very closely to the adaptational problems facing the ancestors at particular times, problems pertaining to diet, social organisation, shelter, defence and the like.[11] At first glance this looks very different to the five-stage model of the evolution of physiomorphic learning adopted here. However, although I have taken issue with Parker and Gibson on some points,[12] our approaches are better considered as complementary than in competition.

It would not be impossible to translate the physiomorphic account into Piagetian terms; the sensori-motor schemata of the versatile early hominid accumulate as its behavioural operations accommodate to an increasing variety of environmental phenomena; this simple proliferation comes to overload the life-routine schemata to which they are being assimilated; a restructuring of cognitive organization ensues. This 'storage reversal' stage might be equated to the abandonment of egocentric thinking in Piaget's developmental sequence. Stage 4 in turn is analogous to the acquisition of 'formal operations', an abstract generalized operation 'To achieve Y identify an X and copy' replacing the 'concrete' situation-specific operations. Such a translation would, though, be both somewhat contrived and obscure the nature of the physiomorphic process itself. A more fruitful way of reconciling the two accounts is to consider the nature of schemata themselves. Certainly the core repertoire of manual and locomotory schemata unfolds more or less according to a biologically determined programme, but once this has matured the repertoire of operations can only expand further by the identification within the environment of novel schemata. In other words the evolution of intelligence, the acquisition of operations of increasing complexity, can only proceed on the basis of an initial perception of such operations as existing in the environment. This will still necessarily appear as a sequence of increasing logical complexity for precisely the same reasons as Piaget's ontogenetic sequence does. The more complex causal relationships holding between environmental phenomena will only be discernible when their simpler components have been understood. Put less technically: in the first place ideas have to come from outside (though once acquired they may be recombined and juxtaposed to generate new ideas in true Lockean fashion).

The structural elaboration of hominid and human cognitive skills, the evolution of intelligence, can only have occurred if the necessary condition of an underlying physiomorphic process was fulfilled. It is this which guarantees that the environmentally located instantiations of the operations which comprise these skills will be attended to and incorporated into the psychological repertoire. The imperative towards structural elaboration of 'intelligence' is itself founded on the deeper epistemological imperative, and this in turn can, on our account, be ultimately traced to pre-existing primate imitative capacities and the consequences for cognitive organization which ensued when these had been exploited to the full.

CONCLUSION

In this chapter I have tried to indicate how the concept of

physiomorphism can be applied to human psychological evolution and the roots of such central cultural phenomena as mythology and religion. Postulating the physiomorphic process as the *central* dynamic provides us with a framework which promises to clarify and integrate a number of problem areas: the origin of culture, the evolution of language, and above all, the origins of human behavioural diversity. Such a perspective does not essentially conflict with accounts such as that of John Crook (1980) (although it should be noted that his assumption of a very early origin of hunting has since fallen from favour). Rather it seeks to identify an underlying psychological dynamic of a very general kind: the relentless, but in a sense blind, incorporation into 'human nature' of Nature itself. This continues until any distinctively species-specific 'human nature' has been effectively lost, to be replaced by socially constructed persons. If accepted, this could, I believe, serve as a background context in which the now quite considerable body of data and theoretical models pertaining to specific aspects of hominid and human evolution can be more meaningfully understood.

CHAPTER SIX

EPILOGUE: THE IMPLODING APE

If this book has a basic message it can be expressed quite simply: the massive global explosion of our species has involved a complementary psychological implosion. With gathering momentum we have succeeded in mastering and incorporating into our psychological and behavioural repertoire the properties and processes we encounter in the outside world. Combining and recombining, analysing and reanalysing these in increasingly complex ways, we have created technologies with which that world has been systematically subordinated to our own anthropocentric ends. We can now even incorporate animal organs into our own bodies – a notion that would have seemed bizarre and repellent science fiction only twenty-five years ago. The world has become a mere 'resource' to be 'consumed'.

The physiomorphic process expresses itself at a number of different levels. Some of these, like tool-use, represent what are initially physiological extensions, a point recognised by McLuhan (1964) when he described media as extensions of the nervous system. But these physiological level phenomena necessarily have a psychological dimension, percolating as it were into the very terms in which we understand ourselves. A cycle has become established in which properties are recombined and re-projected in technological forms which, externalized again, then serve as raw material for re-assimilation. And in the return phase of this cycle the discipline of Psychology plays an increasing part.

An earlier generation saw the central dilemma of 'Modern Man', as it termed us, as located in the conflict between the individual and society, between gratifying our instincts and the demands of civilization, an image shared and articulated by both

Freud and many modern Marxists. This surely now needs reappraising. Technology guarantees gratification; indeed it develops in the service of gratification. Unfortunately the needs it seeks to gratify, doing so by restructuring the external world to cater to such gratifications, do not constitute a logically coherent body of species-specific instinctual demands but a plethora of often mutually exclusive fantasies. The world 'the consumers' are demanding is thus a logically impossible one. The central dilemma is therefore no longer one in which the individual is in conflict with society, but in which society itself is in conflict with logic.

This is a long way from where our argument began, but that we should arrive here was inevitable. It has always been a feature of Psychological theorizing that it reaches a point where its image of the psychological seems to imply a diagnosis of contemporary collective psychopathology, where the theorist feels bound to hold forth on what ails 'the human condition'. Rather than diffidently refraining from drawing such consequences, or merely hinting at them, it is surely preferable and more honest to state clearly what one believes them to be. In this case they appear to be that the physiomorphic strategy *as hitherto enacted* has exhausted its value, and that its further pursuit is only going to get us deeper into the mire of ecological disaster. It is ironic that the organic ecological vision is only emerging (or re-emerging, since it has occured in many different cultures in a variety of forms) at the point when the conditions for its full realization are being destroyed. But this insight (which is indeed a *scientific* one), in the very act of identifying and naming the ecological processes by which the biosphere is maintained, is providing its own raw material for the physiomorphic process. If we can succeed in assimilating this then the old mystical adage that we are a microcosmic reflection of the macrocosm may be given new substance and we may learn to act accordingly.

Was this crisis implicit from the very beginning? Is it a logically necessary outcome of the evolutionary emergence of physiomorphic learning? We are increasingly driven to try and diagnose the point at which things 'began to go wrong'. It is a distressing question, for clearly if we fail to negotiate the current crisis we seem also to retrospectively negate the very achievements on which we have so long prided ourselves. For a Westerner in particular, since Western culture is most centrally implicated in

133

the crisis, the cultural and scientific achievements of the last five hundred years begin to look merely like milestones of illusion. Instead of an ascent we were actually plummeting. What were seen as the outward expressions of 'Man's' high spiritual potential and intrinsically special significance for the universe are transformed into monuments of self-deception, as futile, if also as grandiose, as the furniture in a Pharoah's burial chamber. Those who seek still to affirm the special nobility of what they tend to call 'the human spirit' had better start providing some evidence. Even the most eminent of authorities on human evolution have perenially taken this nobility for granted, and the emergence of *Homo sapiens* from its predecessors has been continually mystified by the insistence that it involved the gratuitously beneficent and inexplicable arrival of some New Ingredient. This might be something as technical as 'capacity for symbolism', or as ethereal as 'reflexive consciousness', or even, for some no doubt, 'an immortal soul'. Even while claiming to elucidate the issue researchers have often, one senses, felt constrained to acknowledge and maintain the notion that something deeply special was involved which will forever resist unmasking. I do not share this orientation. Although the final emergence of language itself is a still tangled issue the broad outline of what has been happening is discernible enough in the account given in the previous chapter. The primate line produced a member who evolved, from existing primate capacities, a form of behavioural amplification which enabled it to successively outflank all ecological checks. It evolved this in response to environmental circumstances which had nothing intrinsically mysterious about them. Once set in motion the process was irreversible; as when life-forms having first gained access to an entirely new niche (like the move from water to land) then proliferate until every nook and cranny has its characteristic fauna and flora, so the exploration of the potentialities of this new learning strategy was unstoppable (and I outlined the way in which this process was structured). It has not been my task in this work to analyse the later phases of human history; to do so would require a far more complex theoretical apparatus in order to explore the ways in which the structure of the human psyche has been affected by the invention of money, the division of labour, industrialization, etc.[1]

Adopting such a theory does not convict me of philistine insensitivity. On the contrary, I have nothing but awe for what my fellow *Homo sapiens* members can achieve and the universes they have created for themselves, including the Einsteinian one. In many of those universes the physiomorphic process was far better understood, and the problems it engendered far more successfully confronted, than is the case today. It is rather that I do not want all this betrayed by a collective refusal to see the problem for what it is. If an image of our condition is needed, then I offer you, in this era of Black Holes, the Imploding Ape.

APPENDIX A: ETYMOLOGICAL SOURCES OF 71 APPARENTLY NON-FIGURATIVE ENGLISH PL WORDS

Word	Origin	Source Classification		
		Non-PL	more ambiguous	PL
ACT	Latin: *agere* = to drive, carry on, do		x	
ANGER	Latin: *angere* = to vex, trouble			x
BEHAVE	*be + have* = 'to have or bear oneself in a specified way'	x		
BELIEF	ultimately from Aryan root *lubh*: to hold dear, valuable, to like		x	
BOLD	Old High German: *bald*			x
BORING	Etymology obscure; OED rejects link with 'hole making'			x
BRAVE	Probably fr. Old Italian: *brado* = wild, savage		x	
CLEVER	Middle English: *clivers* = claws, talons, clutches. 'Nimble of claws, sharp to seize'	x		
COURAGE	Latin: *cor* = heart	x		
DESPAIR	Latin: *de* + *sperare* = hope	x		
DESPISE	Latin: *despicere* = to look down upon	x		
DO	Aryan stem: *dho* = to place, put, set, lay	x		
DOUBT	Latin: *dubius* = waving to and fro	x		
DREAM	Germanic: *draug, drug* = to deceive, delude; 'radical sense being deceptive appearance, illusion'	x		
EMOTION	Latin: *e movere* = out + move	x		
EVIL	Primary sense would be 'exceeding the measure or overstepping the proper limits'; Old Teutonic: *udilo* is root also of *up, over*	x		
EXPLAIN	Latin: *ex* + *planis* = to smooth out, to lay out flat	x		
FANATIC	Latin: *fanum* = temple	x		
FEAR	Old Saxon: *fār* = ambush	x		
FOOLISH	Latin: *follis* = bellows, giving *windbag*, empty-headed person	x		
FREE	Ultimately from Sanskrit root *pri* = to delight, endear, friend		x	

Word	Notes			
FRIEND	See FREE			
FRENZY	Latin: *phrenesis*, from Greek: φρην = midriff. Linked to the use of 'phren' in 'phrenology'. Jaynes (1976) discusses this at length.	x	x	x
FUNNY	Earlier English sense as a verb = to cheat, befool, hoax		x	
FURY	Latin: *furia* = rage, be mad			
GLAD	Old English: *glæd* = smooth			
GRACE	Latin: *gratia* = pleasing quality, attractiveness; OED gives 21 senses in subject (noun) form alone	x	x	
GRATEFUL	Sanskrit: *gurta* = welcome which led also to Greek: γερας = reward	x	x	
GUILT	Origin unknown. Primary sense of 'debt' suggested		x?	x x
HAPPY	Old Danish: *happe* = chance	x	x	
HATE	Old Teutonic: *hatoz* = hate			
HOPE	Old English: *hopa* = hope			
HORROR	Latin: *horrere* = to bristle, shudder	x		
IDEA	Greek: ιδειν = to see, leading to a number of senses such as semblance, form, type, model	x		
INTELLIGENT	Latin: *inter* = between + *legere* = bring together, pick out, choose	x	x	
JEALOUS	Greek: ζηλος = emulation, zeal, jealousy	x		
KIND	Aryan root: *gen, gn* = to produce, engender, beget	x		
KNOW	Ultimately as KIND, but very complex history. Linked to CAN and KEN. More directly derived from Latin: *cognoscere* = to know by the senses.	x		
LOVE	Ultimately from Aryan: *lubh* (see BELIEF)	x	x	
LOYAL	Variant of 'legal'			

139

Word	Origin	Source Classification		
		Non-PL	more ambiguous	PL
LUCK	Gambling term from Old High German: *gelucke*. Ultimate etymology obscure though terms meaning 'to succeed' and 'to entice' have been suggested			x
MAD	Gothic: *gamaips* = crippled. Ultimately from Indo-Germanic root: *mei* = change	x		
MIND	Very complex, incorporating classic terms meaning 'remember', 'intend', 'think', etc. Indo-Germanic root: *men, mon, mn* also occuring widely in e.g. 'mental', 'mnemonic', Greek: μενος = rage etc. Not now believed to be related to MAN (to which OED devotes nearly 5 pages)		x	
NEED	The primary senses of this refer to force, constraint, compulsion, necessity etc.		x	
NOTION	Latin: *noscere* = to know (see KNOW)		x	
PATIENT	Latin: *pati* = to suffer see SUFFER		x	
PLEASANT	The *plac*-root of Latin: *placidus* = mild, gentle and *placare* = calm, smooth (also PLACID, PLACATE)	x		
QUARREL	Latin: *quere* = complain	x		
RAGE	Latin: *rabia* = rabies	x		
REASON	Latin: *rationem* = reckoning, account, etc. Also gives WL terms 'ratio', 'ration'	x		x
RUDE	Latin: *rudis* = unwrought, unformed, inexperienced (all still operative)	x		
SAD	Old Teutonic: *sado* = full, satiated	x		

Word	Notes	15	16	40
SANE	Latin: *sanus* = healthy. But *insanus* always referred to mental condition		x	
SENSE	Latin: *sentire* = to feel			x
SERIOUS	Latin: *serius* = serious	x		
SHAME	Obscure. 'Many scholars assume a Teutonic *skem-* variant of *kem*: to cover, '*covering oneself* being the natural expression of shame.' (OED)	x		x?
SOUL	Ultimate etymology uncertain			
SUFFER	Latin: *sub* + *ferre* = to bear			x
SUSPECT	Latin: *suspectus* = looking up, a height, esteem			x
TERROR	Latin: *terrere* = to frighten			
THANK/THINK/ THOUGHT	Ultimately all from Old Teutonic *þankjan* = to seem, appear. Etymologies of THINK and THOUGHT however are somewhat different in their history prior to fusion as parts of verb TO THINK	x	x	
VAIN	Latin: *vanus* = empty, void, idle			x
WANT	Old Norse: *van-r*: lacking, missing			x
WICKED	Old English: *wicca* = wizard			x
WILL	Sanskrit: *varati* = chooses, wishes, prefers			x
WISE/WIT	Very complex, ultimately from Indo-European: *woid, weid, wid* = to see (to find?) The term Veda (Sanskrit scriptures) and Greek ιδειν (see IDEA) also from this root			x
WISH	Sanskrit: *varati, uen* = to hold dear, love desire			x
WORK	Greek: ειδορ = activity			x
WORRY	Old Friesian: *wergia* = to kill, strangle			x?
WRATH	Possibly linked to Middle High German: *reit, reide* = curled, twisted			x
WRETCHED	Old High German: *recched* = exile, adventurer, knight-errant			
		15	16	40

141

The *Oxford English Dictionary* (1st edn, the 2nd appearing too late for consultation) thus enables us to identify non-PL origins for 40 of these terms and origins which possess a much greater degree of ambiguity or duality of use than the present term in a further 16 cases. This ambiguity is especially evident in the Aryan, Sanskrit, and Indo-Germanic roots such as *lubh, gen, pri, woid* and *men*. This may be interpreted as evidence that many basic PL terms differentiated out of terms which were originally neutral. Fifteen terms are thus unaccounted for: ANGER, BOLD, BORING, DESPAIR, FURY, HATE, HOPE, LUCK, MIND, QUARREL, SERIOUS, SOUL, TERROR, WILL, WISH.

The reasons for failure to identify non-PL roots for this last group are of several kinds; first, there are cases where derivations are given from Classical Greek or Latin source-terms already in PL and not traced back further (ANGER, DESPAIR, FURY, QUARREL, SERIOUS, TERROR); second, there are cases where the OED compilers themselves admit bafflement (BORING, LUCK, SOUL); third, the meaning of Germanic-group source-terms is not always provided – presumably, as with the Classical terms just mentioned, the meanings have remained unchanged and etymology not been traced back further (BOLD, HATE, HOPE). Which leaves MIND and WISH.

In the case of MIND there is an Indo-Germanic root *men* (speculative form), *mon, mn* meaning 'to think, remember, intend'. It is thus in PL as far back as we can go as a term referring in a very general way to psychological activities. WISH is traced back to a Sanskrit base *wen* meaning 'to hold dear, love, desire'. This is similar in definition to the Aryan root *lubh* meaning 'to hold dear, valuable, to like'. The latter however suggests somewhat more ambiguity about whether it is simply a positive approbation term for objects or an emotional term, whilst the former, *wen*, as defined sounds primarily emotional and hence still PL in Sanskrit.

Although no claims for completeness are made for this list it does provide an empirical backing for our central thesis regarding PL generation. None of these terms are recorded as entering the PL vocabulary *de novo*. Where they cannot be traced to non-PL or referentially neutral terms this is because their origins are for one reason or another obscured in the proverbial mists of time.

APPENDIX B: NOTE ON THE STATUS OF THE PHYSIOMORPHIC THEORY

The questions as to what counts as a scientific theory, what the hallmarks of a good scientific theory are, and where the borderlines fall between theories, models, hypotheses, and descriptions are notoriously vexed, and anyone familiar with current debates in philosophy of science will appreciate that consensus on the answers is a long way off. I do not propose entering into these issues here in any depth. A number of points ought nonetheless to be made in relation to the theory, if such it be, being proposed in the present work.

1. A distinction is now frequently made between 'structural' and 'sequential' theories. Although the boundary is, like all boundaries, blurred, this move (proposed by Rychlak 1977) has proved useful in clarifying the different types of account found in the human sciences. Instead of adopting hard Popperian criteria of falsifiability and predictive value it is recognized that such theories as Psychoanalysis and Piagetian genetic epistemology serve a more basic function of providing 'frameworks of meaning'. They define what can occur rather than predict what will actually happen in a given case. They are thus analogous to the Morse Code rule-book or the laws of chess: these do not predict what messages will actually be transmitted or how particular games will be played out, but they define the rules of any transmission or the permissable moves in any game. Structural theories are not empirically falsifiable in any strict sense, their value lies rather in their internal coherence and the quality of the research they stimulate. *Within* a structural theory empirically testable hypotheses can be formulated, but the theory itself defines the terms in which these hypotheses are couched, what counts as

evidence, what counts as falsification, and the like. In such a situation it is not the theory as such that is being tested but hypotheses regarding the details of the operation of the laws and mechanisms which it identifies. Arguably even the most empirically based 'sequential' (deterministic 'cause-and-effect') type theory rests ultimately on a structural framework within which the meanings of its terms are defined and which operates as an axiomatic underpinning of the whole theoretical superstructure.

This last point suggests that the division is not ultimately between types of theory but between complementary features of any theory, theories differing insofar as they seem to weigh more heavily towards one or the other. The physiomorphic theory is, in this respect, in a somewhat intermediate position. Certainly I am seeking to provide a structural account within which the phenomena of the generation and maintenance of PL and human psychological evolution can be construed. On the other hand a number of empirically testable consequences in addition to those proposed towards the end of Chapter 4 do appear to ensue, albeit of a rather general kind.

2. The most important such hypotheses are the following:

i. in relation to Psychological Language:

a) That we will not be able to find a case where a new PL term, identifying novel psychological phenomenon, establishes itself which is not semantically related at some level to non-PL language;
b) That any qualitatively novel external world phenomenon or theoretical concept will in due course acquire a PL meaning;
c) That in articulating their most complex ideas individuals will employ metaphors drawn from their area of maximum expertise;
d) That in formulating their most complex theories Psychologists will employ concepts drawn from those areas of natural science and technology with which they are most familiar;

ii. in relation to human evolution:

a) That no unambiguously 'cultural' artefact will be found

144

preceding the emergence of anatomically modern *Homo sapiens* or the Neanderthals;

b) That the enlargement of the 'language' area in *Homo habilis* did not immediately result in the appearance of language capacities comparable to those of modern humans (this could be established by new evidence regarding their laryngeal anatomy and improved understanding of the cerebral mechanisms governing grammar, which Lieberman (1984) argues are not located in the Broca and Wernicke areas);

c) That when and if a more comprehensive body of empirical data is available for evaluating the growth of the hominid/human behavioural repertoire it will show a saltatory rather than smooth trajectory corresponding to the stages described in Chapter 5;

It is admitted however that rendering these hypotheses into a sufficiently rigorous form to be empirically testable might present problems.

3. In the light of i.d) the present theory itself may be seen to present problems as it is not fundamentally couched in such terms. This is because, in spite of the style in which I have expounded it, it is in important respects a phenomenological account as much as an empirical one. I am in fact acutely conscious that the status of 'physiomorphism' remains, in spite of my efforts, somewhat ambiguous. On the one hand I do wish to insist on its reality as an actual process; that is to say that humans have indeed incorporated into themselves the properties and phenomena of the external world, that there is a genuine dynamic flow from 'outside' to 'inside' from which the 'psychological' is generated. I am not, that is, using the concepts of 'incorporation', 'assimilation' and 'internalization' in a metaphorical sense. Physiomorphic 'incorporation' is not just a question of 'representation'. But equally, in offering this model, it seems to me that I am offering a phenomenological account of how we actually experience ourselves. In its own terms, if the physiomorphic account is accepted, this acceptance has its own psychological effects. There is then a normative level to the account in that I must be claiming 'it is better to look at the situation in these terms', and I am claiming this, in the light of the Epilogue, because it seems to offer

some way of getting a clearer grasp of the nature of the current crisis. Insofar as it has implications for the construal of human evolution, the physiomorphic theory (even of mythology) is, in a technical sense, a myth. This does not worry me too much because the same observation applies to all accounts of origins; the only difference between this and the orthodox heroic 'rise to civilization' yarn around which most scientists still structure their accounts is that I am admitting its mythical dimension.

The absence of any detailed deployment here of current physical science models thus arises from the metatheoretical generality of what I have been aiming for, which has far less use for such models than highly focused analyses of the intricacies of specific psychological processes such as verbal memory or perception. 'Physiomorphism' presents itself therefore as both an image encapsulating a rather general vision of our species 'absorbing' or 'consuming' the world it is in, and as a quite specific learning strategy accounting for our human behavioural diversity and the way in which our psychological identities are socio-historically constructed. The centrality of PL to this theory derives from the fact that it is language which encodes the whole physiomorphic process in a publicly accessible form.

4. The relationship between this theory and the approach currently termed 'Evolutionary epistemology' has been left unexplored in the main text. Its covert influence has been considerable nonetheless, although I find its harder-line expressions somewhat Procrustean in their reductionism of *everything* to a 'random variation and blind selection' (Campbell 1975) schema that requires no further elaboration. The 'five-stage' account of the evolution of physiomorphic learning can though be read in terms of Plotkin and Odling-Smee's 'nested hierarchy of knowledge-gaining processes' (Plotkin and Odling-Smee 1982), and in particular Plotkin's observations regarding the differential rates of change which characterize different modes of knowledge-storage (Plotkin 1987). In general the rate of change accelerates as one proceeds up the hierarchy from genetic to social levels.

My commitment to a fundamentally orthodox view of the sufficiency of the neo-Darwinian account remains fairly strong, but the subtleties of its operation, e.g. in the context of the changing focus of the selection process with the advent of Stage 4, often seem to me to be overlooked. As far as the historical, indeed post-Palaeolithic, phase of our past is concerned, I do not believe we can do without neo-Marxist and modern Psychoanalytic perspectives. This is not because the physiomorphic process ceases but because: a) its cumulative consequences generate new macro-level phenomena in the forms of complex social institutions, cultural products, and economic dynamics; and b) these are themselves recursively internalized as psychic structures. Even so, the underlying dynamic remains the physiomorphic one pictured in Chapter 6.

5. In the final analysis of course the status of the theory cannot be defined by its author. As explained in Chapter 2, in the end meaning is a matter of negotiation. The classic hermeneutic aspiration to reconstruct 'what was really meant', as if the inside of the author's head contains the true objective meaning of what he or she is saying is an illusion. This appendix is merely offering some opening hypotheses as to the terms in which future negotiations, should any be entered into, are to be conducted. This does not mean that we can only retreat into post-Structuralist deconstructionism, since as far as I can understand it this amounts to a refusal to engage in such negotiation at all, adopting, in our terms, a purely Om orientation to texts. Since the meaning of my account of the negotiation of meaning must itself presumably be negotiated, things surely promise to become somewhat tangled.

APPENDIX C:
NOTE ON STONE TOOLS

There has been a very understandable tendency on the part of palaeoarchaeologists and other writers on human evolution to place extraordinarily great significance on stone tool manufacture. Oakley (1981) and Gowlett (1984) both interpret them (at least from the Acheulean on) as implying the presence of high-level psychological operations such as planning, visualization, foresight, even language. Certainly stone-tool manufacture is dramatic evidence of the divergence of the *Homo* lineage from the behavioural repertoire of the pongids (although see Susman 1988). It is worth considering however if we may not be making a serious error here. Do not the extremely slow pace of their evolution and their homogeneity of design prior to the demise of *H. erectus* suggest that we are dealing with something far more akin to the species-specific genetically-based 'tool-making' and 'tool-use' skills which have occasionally emerged among other species than with a consciously planned technology? My own suspicion is that making stone tools was an almost direct consequence of the utilization of pre-existing manual operations present in a non-ground-dwelling primate ancestor vis-à-vis the stones present in the new environment (see Richards 1986). As suggested in the main text, utilization of the properties of broken stone is a prime example of physiomorphic assimilation. But, perhaps arguing slightly against myself here, I suspect that it may have been one of the very few distinctively species-specific, in part genetically-based (at least 'prepared') items in the proto-hominid repertoire. That it later provided one basis for technological evolution I would not of course dispute. Because stone tools were for so long effectively the only surviving evidence of early hominid

148

behaviour available to researchers – a single 'figure' against a 'ground' of silence – their actual role may well have been somewhat exaggerated, or at least been given a more simple and dramatic character, than is really justified (see also Richards 1989).

NOTES

INTRODUCTION

1 Monod J. (1972); see particularly pp.37-9
2 In no case may we interpret an action as the outcome of the exercise of a higher psychical faculty, if it can be interpreted as the outcome of the exercise of one which stands lower in the psychological scale(1894:53).
This he reiterated in 1900 as:

> we should not interpret animal behaviour as the outcome of higher mental processes, if it can be fairly explained as due to the operation of those which stand lower in the psychological scale of development. (1900:270)

Alan Costall (1987) has persuasively argued that Lloyd Morgan's intentions in formulating the Canon were somewhat different from those now usually ascribed to it. Arising in the context of a debate with George Romanes, the object of the Canon was, Costall argues, to leave room for judiciously disciplined 'anthropomorphism' rather than to excommunicate all non-humans from the realm of the psychological.
3 Pasteur's discovery of the active role of yeast in the conversion of sugar to alcohol was contrary to the orthodox view (notably of Liebig) that it was purely catalytic. This led on to open up the whole area of microbiology, taking in *en route* the settling of the 'spontaneous generation' issue and eventually facilitating the discovery of the biochemical nature and function of enzymes.
4 I have adopted this distinction throughout the book hence the reader should remain alert to the difference between phrases and terms such as 'impact on psychology' and 'impact on Psychology', 'psychological' and 'Psychological' etc.

CHAPTER 1

1 see Lubbock (6th edn, 1912) *Prehistoric Times*, p. 361.

2 This is Thomas Traherne's (d. 1684) translation in his 'Centuries' (Fourth Century, 76). Originally published in 1487, *On the Dignity of Man* was issued in a modern translation (by Wallis) New York, Bobbs-Merrill, 1965.

3 see William James (1890) *Principles of Psychology*.

4 This paper is extremely important for an understanding of the current anthropological perspective on the issues discussed here. Classification has of course been a central concern of anthropology since Durkheim and Mauss's 1903 essay 'De Quelques Formes Primitives de Classification' (translated and edited by Rodney Needham as *Primitive Classification*, 1963).

5 It should be stressed here that Ellen's paper is not primarily concerned with PL generation but with arguing for the primacy of the human body as a basis for classification in general:

> My contention is simply that the human body forms the concrete basis of a characteristic classificatory apparatus for parts ordered analytically, which acts as a primary constraint in structuring 'cognitive meshes', and that this is not obliterated by the process of cultural re-organization, since the very mechanism of the process is itself partially constrained by it. . . .In one sense it is true that body classification is not arbitrary: cognitive structures are, indeed, extensions of biological structures, but they are at the same time discovered through the process of cultural and social interaction. The process of classification may be visualised as operating at two coexisting and interpenetrating levels, represented by the analytic and the synthetic. At the first level, structures may be regarded as 'deep', dominant ones being determined by a combination of material constraints and cerebral apparatus, and influence of the cultural is superficial only in terms of providing lexical labels for culturally defined material parts. . . . While the body, as with all nature, may be redefined and reified in cultural terms, it is not in the first instance of perception defined as such: the classification itself takes on a concretised form.
>
> (Ellen 1977:369)

In fact much of Ellen's account seems to be quite consistent with the argument, to be put forward in Chapter 3, that basic sensory and motor behaviour provide a core of pre-cultural PL schemata.

6 R. Willis (1974) provides a comparative study of three African peoples: the Nuer, the Lele, and the Fipa. In each of these cultures a particular animal (ox, pangolin, and python respectively) plays a central symbolic role. Willis gives us an intriguing and complex analysis of the way in which this role emerges from the central values and social structures of these cultures. These are also reflected in their respective village layouts: the Lele living in highly-ordered rectilinear

. villages, for example, while the Fipa huts are 'scattered higgledy-piggledy' and their 'overall plan tends to be circular' (1974:41); the Nuer practise a climatically-determined twice-yearly migration, alternating between a nomadic life-style and an 'annual contraction' into isolated villages which function as an 'economic corporation' with commonly-owned facilities (1974:61).

CHAPTER 2

1 In order to present the necessarily somewhat tortuous argument of this chapter as straightforwardly as possible I have minimized the number of references to other work in the field.
2 I am aware that computer simulation of language use can go beyond this; as long ago as 1970, Winograd's SHRDLU program for instance could state which items must be moved to get access to others. Nevertheless this does not, I believe, undermine the argument in the rest of the paragraph that language is used to mediate the social relationships etc. of a community of language users.
3 Which is not to deny that individual humans at various points consciously introduced specific innovations *within* it.
4 An earlier version of this triad, in its 'linguistic role' aspect, is the US pragmatist C. S. Pierce's trio of Sign, Signified, and Interpreter (see Gallie 1952). I am indebted to Robert Lowe for drawing this to my attention. Some integration of the present account with Peirce's general theory of signs is clearly required. Another of his triads, doubt, certainty, and inquiry, also needs resuscitating, though I would suggest that it omits a fourth and essential term: indifference!

CHAPTER 3

1 This is sometimes claimed to have originated in an event in Medieval history in which the occupants of a besieged town hung out a live goose on the ramparts to mock their assailants. Brewer (1895) has Eric, King of Sweden involved in a somewhat more complicated episode, riposting that he wanted 'To cook your goose for you' in reply to the enemy's enquiries as to his intentions in this situation. This now seems to have been rejected, so nobody is really sure of its origins.
2 The *ba* or 'heart-soul' (something like 'life-force') is depicted as a jabiru stork, but according to Budge (1928) it could also be depicted as a human-headed hawk (1928:1x), while the *akh*, or 'spiritual soul', is depicted as a crested ibis. (Many of Budge's phonetics were actually abandoned about seventy years ago – he calls the *akh, khu*; thanks to Ms Andrews of the British Museum, Department of Egyptian Antiquities, for putting me right on this and identifying the first and last of the species.)

3 Whether the original is actually in such a rhetorical tone is a moot point; the original English translation (Pliny, 1601) is far more sober:

> This element of Fire is infinit, and never ceaseth to be working, insomuch, as it is hard to say whether it consume more than it engendereth.
>
> (Book 36, Chap.xxvi, p.599)

The Latin is:

> immensa, inproba rerum naturæ et in qua dubium sit, plura absumat an pariat
>
> (C. Mayhoff ed. 1977)

4 The giving of proper names, on the other hand, frequently (though not always) involves the identification of the named with a natural phenomenon. Females are often given plant names (*Rose, Jasmine, Myrtle, Ivy, Daisy,* and *Violet,* etc.); the wolf has yielded *Wulf, Wolfgang, Wolfram (wolf-raven!), Ulfric,* and the surnames *Wolsey, Woolmer,* and *Woolgar; Everard* and *Ewart* are from *Eber,* a mythic Teutonic boar; while *Arnold* and *Bernard* originate in a mythological eagle and bear respectively. Indeed the Saxons, Teutons, and Norsemen had a great penchant for calling their offspring names meaning things like 'bright wolf' (*Bardolf*), 'eagle cauldron' (*Arnkatla*), 'bear fury' (*Bjornheddin*), and 'raven spear' (*Ravengar*) (all these are taken from Yonge 1863). A full analysis of proper-naming practices would require a book in itself, but it is fairly clear that one of the basic strategies for giving ourselves personal identities is to be formally identified with a specific feature of our environment in this way. See also Bean (1980) for a useful review of this topic from an ethnological perspective.

CHAPTER 4

1 A more comprehensive review of this will be undertaken in the present writer's *Mental Machinery: A History of Psychological Ideas from 1600 to the Present Day,* currently in preparation for Athlone Press.
2 Thomas Willis's most significant work for historians of Psychology is his *Cerebri Anatome* of 1664 (illustrated by Christopher Wren, no less); this was translated into English by Samuel Pordage in 1681 along with other works by him and then republished in 1684 in a volume containing all of Willis's writings. The 1681 edition of the *Anatomy of the Brain and Nerves* was reprinted in facsimile in 1965 (W. Feindel (ed.), Montreal, McGill University Press). The text is the same in both 1681 and 1684 editions but the pagination differs. Quotes in the text are from the 1681 edition. The work '*On Fermentation or the Inorganical Motion of Natural Bodies*' opens both publications. *Two Discourses concerning the Soul of Brutes, which is that of the Vital and Sensitive of Man,* another important essay by Willis, is included in the 1684 edition. Not all the imagery is chemical or mechanical of course:

Having hitherto continued the former Tract of the oblong
Marrow, which as it were the Kings High-way, leades from the
Brain, as the Metropolis, into many Provinces of the nervous
stock, by private recesses and cross-ways; it follows now that we
view the other City of the animal Kingdom. The situation of this
being remote enough from the former, its kind of structure is
also different from it: yea it seems that there are granted to this,
as to a free and municipal City, certain Priviledges and a peculiar
Jurisdiction.

(1684:90)

3 The full impact of the mechanical vision comes in the eighteenth
century and various aspects of it have now received academic
attention. Wimsatt's (1948) classic study of Samuel Johnson's use of
'philosophic words' has been followed more recently by several essay
collections containing relevant papers: Boucé, P.-G.(ed.)(1982) on
sexuality; V. G. Myer (ed.) (1984) on Sterne; and Benjamin, A. E. *et al*
(eds) (1987) being particularly apposite. See also G. S. Rousseau
(1980). Chapter 1 of Wimsatt (1948) is important for the seventeenth
century situation also, suggesting that the impoverishment of PL in
philosophical texts did not entirely reflect the reality: 'Such words as
elasticity, intensity, polarity, static, or *volatile* may be readily detected
moving from the literal scientific realm to the metaphoric and
psychological' (1968 edn:14)
4 OED (4) gives this sense of emotion ('Any agitation or disturbance of
mind, feeling, passion; any vehement or excited mental state') as
appearing first in 1660, quoting Jeremy Taylor 'The emotions of
humanity...the meltings of a worthy disposition'.
5 See C. Hill (1972), esp. Chapter 16 and Appendix A; see also Hodgen
(1964) on the impact of geographical discoveries and encounters with
diverse tribal cultures on views of human nature in the sixteenth and
seventeenth centuries.
6 His statement that 'the founding moments of psychology always
concern the pathological' (Rose 1985:22) may though be disputed.
J. N. Tetens' (1777) *Philosophische Versuche über die menschliche Natur
und ihre Entwicklung* is seriously being argued to be the founding text
of developmental Psychology and does not primarily concern
pathology (see P. B. Baltes 1983).
7 See, in addition to Harte, Milne Bramwell (1913), and an intriguing
paper by Pulos (1980).
8 Of course magnets had been known for centuries (especially by the
Chinese), but aside from Gilbert's isolated *De Magnete* (1600) it is only
in the eighteenth century that magnetism and electrical phenomena
begin to receive the systematic attention from scientists that could
generate genuinely novel WL concepts regarding their nature.
9 B. Mackenzie's *Behaviourism and the Limits of Scientific Method* (1977) is
perhaps the best critical study of the theoretical foundations of

Watsonian Behaviorism.

10 See Ehrenreich and English (1979) for entertaining coverage of his influence in this direction and an account of the 'externalist' background to Watson's rise to influence in the USA.

11 The kindergarten class attended by the infant Gauss was asked by the teacher to add up 1+2+3+4...up to +10. Gauss immediately raised his hand up with the answer – 55. Asked how he did it so quickly he allegedly replied to the effect that 1+10=11, 2+9=11...; there being five such pairs the answer must be 5x11=55. Wertheimer used this to illustrate the effects of the way a problem is structured on the ease of its solution (see Wertheimer 1961, Chapter 4).

12 It was during this period that their work began to receive wide attention; the ethological movement itself dated back to pre-World War Two work by Uexkull and Tinbergen.

CHAPTER 5

1 One recent paper (McGrew 1987) goes so far as to claim that, in terms of formal analysis, the subsistence technology levels of Tasmanian aborigines and Tanzanian chimpanzees are highly similar, although only the former use artefacts incorporating more than one 'technounit' (i.e. more than one kind of raw material) – even so, the actual size of the 'subsistence tool-kits' is almost identical: 13 in the human one versus 12 in the chimpanzee one.

2 This is discussed by Marshack (1977) who sees the engraved meanders as comparable in 'cognitive strategy' to some of those found on much later ivory plaques and engraved bones. Whether or not this artefact (and the ochre-use evidence from Terra Amata) should be interpreted as really 'cultural' is a moot point. Marshack's general interpretation of this widespread Upper Palaeolithic genre was that it constituted some form of 'iconographic participation' with water. This is obviously highly suggestive in the context of the ideas being proposed here. As far as the Pêche de l'Aze ox-rib itself is concerned, it remains so temporally isolated and enigmatic that nothing can be firmly ascertained from it. In terms of the stages in the evolution of physiomorphic learning proposed in this chapter there is no clear reason for allocating its makers to a Stage 5 rather than a Stage 4 level.

3 100,000 years being the approximate age of both the Border Cave, South Africa and Qafzeh, Israel remains (see Valladas et al. 1988).

4 I have reviewed this evidence in Richards 1987b.

5 See Richards (1989) for a further account of this.

6 See Richards (1987b) Chapter 5 for a summary of these various 'ding-dong', 'bow-wow', 'sing-song', etc. accounts.

7 See Introduction, pp. 4–5

8 See also Brenda E. E. Beck (1978). While finding both of these papers stimulating I find it difficult to integrate the technical terms of their anthropological discourse into my own discussion. It is clear that

anthropological analysis of metaphor and metonymy has elaborated many of the topics I have been touching on in great detail; nevertheless, they have by and large accepted metaphor as an unproblematic concept in itself, and do not appear to have addressed psychological discourse, PL, as a specific topic for investigation.

9 The following passage from *Aristotle's Masterpiece*, a best-selling sex manual for over two centuries (it first appeared in 1684, and went through 32 editions in the US alone between 1766 and 1831) is quoted by Boucé (1982), (needless to say Aristotle had nothing to do with it):

> Partridges, Quails, Sparrows, etc. being extreamly addicted to Venery, they work the same Effect in those who eat them: And this likewise is worthy to be noted, That what Part of the Body the Faculty that you would strengthen lies, take the same Part of another Creature, in whom that Faculty is strong, as a Medicine.
>
> (Boucé, 1982:38)

I recall a deep-sea fisherman once recommending the tail of cod, as it was 'the tail that guides the cod'. It did not seem prudent to reply 'yes, but into a net'.

10 J. D. Lewis-Williams (1983) has revolutionized the understanding of South African 'San' rock art by using this perspective. See M. W. Conkey (1987) for a recent review of 'Palaeolithic Art'.

11 See Richards 1987b, Chapter 4 for a critical summary.

12 See Richards 1987b, pp. 172-87.

CHAPTER 6

1 In this connection I have been impressed by the work of the Marxist Psychoanalyst Bornemann (1976), particularly his essay on 'The Midas Complex'.

REFERENCES

Allegro, John (1973), *The Sacred Mushroom and the Cross*, London: Abacus.

Allport, G. W. and Odbert, H. S. (1936), 'Trait-names: a psycho-lexical study', *Psychological Monographs* 47:1-171; No. 211.

Attar, Farid Ud-Din, (trans. C. S. Nott) (1985), *The Conference of the Birds*, London: Arkana.

Austin, John (1962), How To Do Things With Words, Oxford: Clarendon Press.

Bakan, D. (1975), *Sigmund Freud and the Jewish Mystical Tradition*, New York: Beacon.

Baltes, P. B. (1983), 'Life-span developmental psychology: observations on history and theory revisited', in R. M. Lerner (ed.) *Developmental Psychology: Historical and Philosophical Perspectives*, New York: Erlbaum.

Bean, Susan B. (1980), 'Ethnology and the study of proper names', *Anthropological Linguistics*, October, pp. 305-16.

Beck, Brenda E. E. (1978), 'The metaphor as a mediator between semantic and analogic modes of thought', *Current Anthropology* 19(1): 83-97.

Benjamin, A. E., Cantor, G. N. and Christie J. R. R. (eds) (1987), *The Figural and the Literal: Problems of Language in the History of Science and Philosophy, 1630-1800*, Manchester: Manchester University Press.

Bennington, Geoff (1987), 'The perfect cheat: Locke and empiricism's rhetoric', in Benjamin, A. E. *et al.* (eds) (1987), pp. 103-23.

Berkeley, G. (1710), *The Principles of Human Knowledge*, London: Collins; reprinted 1962.

Blumenberg, B. (1983), 'The evolution of the advanced hominid brain', *Current Anthropology*, 24 (5) 589-623.

Bornemann, E. (ed.) (1976), *The Psychoanalysis of Money*, London: Pluto Press.

Boucé, P.-G. (1982), 'Some sexual beliefs and myths in eighteenth-century Britain', in Boucé, P.-G. (ed.), *Sexuality in Eighteenth-Century Britain*, Manchester: Manchester University Press, pp. 28-46.

Brainerd, C. J. (1978), 'The stage question in cognitive-developmental

157

theory', *Behavioural and Brain Sciences*, 1 (2) 173–214.

Brewer, E. Cobham (1895), *Dictionary of Phrase and Fable*, London: Cassell.

Bromley, D. B.(1977), *Personality Description in Ordinary Language*, Chichester: Wiley.

Brown, Cecil H. (1979), 'Folk-zoological life-forms: their universality and growth', *American Anthropologist* 81 (4): 791-817.

Brown, Cecil H. and Witkowski, S. R. (1981), 'Figurative language in a universalist perspective', *American Ethnologist* 8(3): 596-615.

Budge, E. A. Wallis (1928), *The Book of the Dead*, London: Kegan Paul Trench & Trübner.

Burton, R. (1624) (ed. A. R. Shilleto 1896), *The Anatomy of Melancholy* (3 vols), London: George Bell & Sons.

Campbell, D. T. (1975), 'On the conflicts between biological and social evolution and between psychology and moral tradition', *American Psychologist*, December, pp. 1103-26.

Campbell, Joseph (1984), *The Way of the Animal Powers*, London: Times Books.

Chaucer, G. (ed. R. Morris 1893), *The Parlement of Briddes or the Assembly of Foules*, in *The Poetical Works of Geoffrey Chaucer* Vol.6, London: George Bell.

Collins, A. M. and Quillian, M. R. (1969), 'Retrieval time from semantic memory', *Journal of Verbal Learning and Verbal Behaviour* 8: 240-7.

Conkey, M. W. (1987), 'New approaches in the search for meaning? A review of research in "Paleolithic Art"', *Journal of Field Archaeology* 14: 413-30.

Costall, A. (1987), 'Before the Canon: Lloyd Morgan on the possibility of a Comparative Psychology', Paper given at the 1st Annual Conference of the History and Philosophy Section of the British Psychological Society, Ilkley College, 22-24 April 1987.

Crook, J (1980), *The Evolution of Human Consciousness*, Oxford: OUP.

Danziger, K. (1983), 'Origins of the schema of stimulated motion: towards a pre-history of modern psychology', *History of Science* xxi: 183-210.

Darwin, C. (1871), *The Descent of Man*, London: John Murray; 2nd edn, 1874.

Davies, Tony (1987), 'The Ark in flames: science, language and education in seventeenth-century England' in Benjamin, A. E. *et al.* (eds) (1987), pp. 83-102.

Dennis, W. (ed.) (1948), *Readings in the History of Psychology*, New York: Appleton-Century-Crofts.

De Saussure, F. (1916), *Course in General Linguistics*, London: Fontana; reprinted 1974.

Descartes, R. (1650) *Passions of the Soul*, in Dennis, W. (ed.) (1948) *Readings in the History of Psychology*, New York: Appleton-Century-Crofts.

Desmond, A. (1979), *The Ape's Reflexion*, London: Blond and Briggs.

Durkheim, E. and Mauss, M. (trans. R. Needham) (1963), *Primitive*

Classification, London: Cohen & West.

Ehrenreich, B. and English, D. (1979), *For Her Own Good – A Century of the Experts' Advice to Mothers*, New York: Pluto Press.

Ellen, Roy F. (1977), 'Anatomical classification and the semiotics of the body', in John Blacking (ed.), *The Anthropology of the Body*, ASA Monograph 15, London, New York, and San Francisco: Academic Press.

Evans-Pritchard, Sir E. (ed. A. Singer) (1981), *A History of Anthropological Thought*, London: Faber and Faber.

Eysenck, H. J. (1986), *The Decline and Fall of the Freudian Empire*, Harmondsworth: Penguin.

Farrington, B. (1961), *Greek Science: Its Meaning for Us*, Harmondsworth: Penguin.

Fernandez, James (1974), 'The mission of metaphor in expressive culture', *Current Anthropology* 15 (2): 119-45.

Fox, R. (1979), 'The evolution of mind: an anthropological approach', *Journal of Anthropological Research* 35 (2): 138-56.

Frazer, J. (1890–1936), *The Golden Bough* (13 volumes), London: Macmillan.

French, R. K. (1969), *Robert Whytt, The Soul and Medicine*, London: Wellcome Institute of the History of Medicine.

Freud, S. (1910) (trans. J. Strachey, 1957), *Five Lectures on Psycho-Analysis*, in *Standard Edition of Freud's Works*, XI, London: Hogarth Press and the Institute of Psycho-Analysis.

Gallie, W. B. (1952), *Peirce and Pragmatism*, Harmondsworth: Penguin Books.

Gert, B. (1986), 'Wittgenstein's Private Language Arguments', *Synthese* 68: 409-39.

Gerwitz, J. L. and Stingle, K. G. (1968), 'Learning of generalised imitation as the basis for identification', *Psychological Review* 25 (5): 374-97.

Gilbert, W. (1600) *De Magnete*, London.

Govinda, Lama Anagarika (1961), *The Psychological Attitude of Early Buddhist Philosophy and its Systematic Representation according to Abhidhamma Tradition*, London: Rider.

Gowlett, J. A. J. (1984), 'Mental abilities of early man: a look at some hard evidence', in R. Foley (ed.) *Hominid Evolution and Community Ecology*, London: Academic Press, pp.167-97.

Griaule, M. (1965), *Conversations with Ogotemmêli: An Introduction to Dogon Religious Ideas*, London: Oxford University Press.

Hall, Spencer T. (ed.) (1843), *The Phreno-Magnet and Mirror of Nature: A Record of Facts, Experiments, and Discoveries in Phrenology, Magnetism, etc.*, London: Simpkin, Marshall & Co.

Harte, R. (1902), *Hypnotism and the Doctors, Vol. 1: Mesmer, De Puységur*, London: L. N. Fowler.

Hewes, G. W. (1973), 'An explicit formulation of the relationship between tool-using, tool-making, and the emergence of language', *Visible Language* 7(2): 101-27.

Hewitt, J. (1960), *Teach Yourself Yoga*, London: English Universities Press.

Hill, C. (1964), 'William Harvey and the Ideal of Monarchy', *Past and Present: A Journal of Historical Studies*. 27: 54–72.

—— (1972; rep. 1975 by Penguin Books), *The World Turned Upside Down: Radical Ideas during the English Revolution*, London: Maurice Temple Smith.

Hobbes, T. (1651), *Leviathan or the Matter, Forme and Power of a Commonwealth, Ecclesiastical and Civil*, London.

Hodgen, M. T. (1964), *Early Anthropology in the Sixteenth and Seventeenth Centuries*, Philadelphia: University of Pennsylvania Press; reprinted 1971.

Holloway, R. L. (1981), 'Culture, symbols and brain evolution', *Dialectical Anthropology* 5: 287-303.

Höffding, Harald (1891), *Outlines of Psychology*, London, Macmillan.

Hooke, R. (1665), *Micrographia*, London: J. Martyn and J. Allestry for the Royal Society.

Itard, J. M. G. (1801), *De L'Education d'un homme sauvage ou des premiers dévelopments physiques et moreaux du jeune sauvage de l'Aveyron*, Paris: Gouyon.

James. W. (1890), *Principles of Psychology*, New York: Henry Holt.

Jaynes, J. (1976), *The Origin of Consciousness in the Breakdown of the Bicameral Mind*, New York: Houghton Mifflin.

Kelly, G. A. (1955), *The Psychology of Personal Constructs* (2 vols), New York: Norton.

Koffka, K. (1935), *Principles of Gestalt Psychology*, New York: Harcourt Brace.

Kuper, Adam (1988), *The Invention of Primitive Society*, London: Routledge.

Lakoff, G. and Johnson, M. (1980), *Metaphors We Live By*, Chicago and London: University of Chicago Press.

Lane, H. (1979), *The Wild Boy of Aveyron*, London: Paladin.

Lauder Lindsay, W. (1880), *Mind in the Lower Animals* (2 vols), London: Kegan Paul Trench.

Lévi-Strauss, C. (1966), *The Savage Mind*, London: Weidenfeld & Nicolson; reprinted 1972.

Lewis-Williams, J. D. (1983), *Rock Art of Southern Africa*, Cambridge: Cambridge University Press.

Lieberman, P. (1984), *The Biology and Evolution of Language*, Cambridge, Mass. and London: Harvard University Press.

Lloyd Morgan, C. (1894), *Introduction to Comparative Psychology*, London: Arnold.

—— (1900), *Animal Behaviour*, London: Arnold.

Lonsdale, Steven (1981), *Animals and the Origins of Dance*, London: Thames & Hudson.

Locke, J. (1689, rep. ed. A. S. Pringle-Pattison 1964), *An Essay Concerning Human Understanding*, Oxford: Clarendon Press.

Lubbock, J. [Lord Avebury] (6th edn, 1912), *Prehistoric Times*, London:

Williams & Norgate.

Mackenzie, B. (1977), *Behaviourism and the Limits of Scientific Method*, London: Routledge & Kegan Paul.

McGrew, W. C. (1987), 'Tools to get food: the subsistants of Tasmanian aborigines and Tanzanian chimpanzees compared', *Journal of Anthropological Research*: 247-58.

McLuhan, M. (1964), *Understanding Media: the Extensions of Man*, London: Routledge & Kegan Paul.

Marshack, A. (1972), *The Roots of Civilization*, New York: McGraw-Hill, and London: Wiley.

—— (1977), 'The meander as a system: the analysis and recognition of iconographic units in Upper Palaeolithic compositions' in P. J. Ucko (ed.) *Form in Indigenous Art*, Canberra: Australian Institute of Aboriginal Studies.

Midgley, M. (1979), 'Brutality and sentimentality', *Philosophy* 54:385-9.

Milne Bramwell, J. (1913), *Hypnotism: Its History, Practice and Theory*, London: William Rider; reprinted 1921.

Mischel, W. (1973), 'Toward a cognitive social learning reconceptualization of personality', *Psychological Review* 80:252-83.

Moncalm, M. (trans. G. S. Whitmarsh) (1905), *The Origin of Thought and Speech*, London: Kegan Paul Trench & Trübner.

Monod, J. (1972), *Chance and Necessity*, London: Collins.

Müller, F. M. (1887), *The Science of Thought*, London: Longman.

Myer, V. G. (ed.) (1984), *Laurence Sterne: Riddles and Mysteries*, London: Vision Press, and Totowa, New Jersey: Barnes & Noble.

Nakamura, T. (1977), 'T. Willis' and Lower's physiology with special reference to the theory of heart movement', *Japanese Studies in the History of Science* 16:23-41.

Ninio, A. (1986), 'The illocutionary aspect of utterances', *Discourse Processes* 9:127-47.

Oakley, K. P. (1981), 'Emergence of higher thought 3.00 – 0.2 Ma B.P.', *Philosophical Transactions of the Royal Society of London*, B292, pp. 205-11.

Parker, S. T. and Gibson, K. R. (1979), 'A developmental model for the evolution of language and intelligence in early hominids', *The Behavioural and Brain Sciences*, 2: 367-408.

Peters, R. S. (1964), *The Concept of Motivation*, London: Routledge & Kegan Paul.

Pliny the Elder (trans. Philemon Holland) (1601), *The Historie of the World Commonly called the Naturall Historie of C. Plinius Secundus*, London: Andrew Islip.

—— (ed. C. Mayhoff) (1977; 1st edn 1897), *C. Plini Secundi, Naturalis Historæ* Stuttgart: Teubner.

Plotkin, H. C. (1987), 'Evolutionary epistemology and the synthesis of biological and social sciences' in W. Callebaut and R. Pinxten (eds), *Evolutionary Epistemology: A Multiparadigm Program*, Dordrecht: D. Reidel.

Plotkin, H. C. and Odling-Smee, F. J. (1982), 'Learning in the context of a hierarchy of knowledge gaining processes', in H. C. Plotkin (ed.), *Learning, Development and Culture: Essays in Evolutionary Epistemology*, Chichester: John Wiley, pp. 443-71.

Porta, Giovanni Battista della (1586), *De Humana Physiognomia Libri IIII*, Apud J. Cacchium: Vici Aequensis.

Pribram, K. (1980), 'The Role of Analogy in Transcending Limits in the Brain Sciences', *Daedalus*, 109 (2): 19-38.

Price, A. F. & Wong Mou-lam (trans.)(1969), *The Diamond Sutra and The Sutra of Hui Neng*, Berkeley CA: Shambhala.

Pulos, Lee (1980), 'Mesmerism Revisited: The Effectiveness of Esdaile's Techniques in the Production of Deep Hypnosis and Total Body Hypnoanaesthesia', *American Journal of Clinical Hypnosis* 22 (4): 206-11.

Rapaport, D. (1960), *The Structure of Psychoanalytic Theory: A Systematizing Attempt*, New York: International Universities Press, (*Psychological Issues*, II (2): Monograph 6).

Reiss, T. J. (1982), *The Discourse of Modernism*, Ithaca and London: Cornell University Press.

Richards, G. D. (1986), 'Freed hands or enslaved feet? A note on the behavioural implications of ground-dwelling bipedalism', *Journal of Human Evolution* 15: 143-50.

—— (1987a), 'Of what is the history of psychology a history?', *British Journal for the History of Science*, 20 (2): 201-11.

—— (1987b), *Human Evolution: An Introduction for the Behavioural Sciences*, London: Routledge & Kegan Paul.

—— (1989), 'Human behavioural evolution: a physiomorphic model', *Current Anthropology* 30(2): 244-55.

Rivers, W. H. R. (1926), 'The primitive conception of death'; published as Chapter 3 of *Psychology and Ethnology*, London: Kegan Paul.

Robins, R. H.(1967), *A Short History of Linguistics*, London: Longmans.

Romanyshyn, R. D. (1982), *Psychological Life: from Science to Metaphor*, Milton Keynes: Open University Press.

Rose, N. (1985), *The Psychological Complex: Psychology, Politics and Society in England 1869-1939*, London: Routledge & Kegan Paul.

Ross, G. M. (1988), 'Hobbes and Descartes on the relation between language and consciousness', *Synthese* 75: 217-29.

Rousseau, G. S. (1980), 'Psychology', in G. S. Rousseau and Roy Porter (eds), *The Ferment of Knowledge*, Cambridge: Cambridge University Press, pp. 143-210.

Rychlak, J. (1977), *The Psychology of Rigorous Humanism*, NY etc.: Wiley.

Ryle, Gilbert (1949), *The Concept of Mind*, London: Hutchinson.

Sampson, Geoffrey (1980), *Schools of Linguistics: Competition and Evolution*, London: Hutchinson.

Samarin, William, J. (1979), 'Making sense of glossolalic nonsense', *Social Research* 46 (1): 88-105.

Schrödinger, Erwin (1967), *What is Life? and Mind and Matter*, Cambridge: Cambridge University Press.

Searle, John (1969), *Speech Acts*, Cambridge: Cambridge University Press.

Sellars, W. (1980), 'Behaviorism, Language and Meaning', *Pacific*

Philosophical Quarterly 61 (1-2): 3-25.

Sève, L. (1978), *Man in Marxist Theory and the Psychology of Personality*, Brighton: Harvester Press.

Sheldon W. H. (1954), *Atlas of Men: A Guide for Somatotyping the Adult Male at All Ages*, New York: Harper.

Sieveking, A. (1979), *The Cave Artists*, London: Thames & Hudson.

Spence, K. W. (1938), 'Gradual vs. sudden solution of discrimination problems by chimpanzees', *Journal of Comparative Psychology* 25: 213-24.

Suarez, S. D. and Gallup, G. G. (1981), 'Self recognition in chimpanzees and orangutans but not gorillas', *Journal of Human Evolution* 110: 175-88.

Susman, R. L. (1988), 'Hand of *Paranthropus robustus* from Member I, Swartkrans: Fossil evidence for tool behavior', *Science* 240: 781-4.

Swift, J. (1726-7), *Travels into Several Remote Nations of the World by Lemuel Gulliver*, London.

Tetens, J. N. (1777), *Philosophische Versuche über die menschliche Natur und ihre Entwicklung*, Leipzig: Weidmanns Erben & Reich.

Valladas, H. *et al.* (1988), 'Thermoluminescence dating of Mousterian 'Proto-Cro-Magnon' remains from Israel and the origin of modern man', *Nature* 331: 614-16.

Villas Boas, O. and C. (1974), *Xingu: The Indians and their Myths*, London: Souvenir Press.

Waismann, F. (1953), 'Language Strata' in A. G. N. Flew (ed.), *Logic and Language (2nd Series)*, Oxford: Blackwell.

Walker, Stephen (1983), *Animal Thought*, London: Routledge & Kegan Paul.

Watson, J. B. (1913), 'Psychology as the behaviorist views it', *Psychological Review*, XX: 158-77.

—— (1924), *Behaviorism*, New York: Norton; reprinted 1970.

—— (1928), *Psychological Care of Infant and Child*, New York: W. W. Norton.

Webster, C. (ed.) (1974), *The Intellectual Revolution of the Seventeenth Century*, London: Routledge & Kegan Paul.

Weiss, A. P. (1925), *A Theoretical Basis of Human Behavior*, Columbus, Ohio: Adams.

Wertheimer, M. (1961), *Productive Thinking*, London: Tavistock Publications.

Whitney, William Dwight (2nd edn, 1876), *The Life and Growth of Language*, London: Henry S. King.

Whitteridge, G. (1971), *William Harvey and the Circulation of the Blood*, London: MacDonald.

Wilhelm, R. (trans.) (1984), *The Secret of the Golden Flower*, London: Arkana.

Wilkins, John (1668), *An Essay Towards a Real Character and a Philosophical Language*, London: Gellibrand & Martin for the Royal Society.

Williams, L. (1980), *The Dancing Chimpanzee: A Study on the Origins of Primitive Music*, London: Alison & Busby.

Willis, Roy (1974), *Man and Beast*, London: Hart-Davis, MacGibbon.

Willis, Thomas (trans. S. Pordage) (1681; rep. 1684), *The Anatomy of the Brain*, in *The Remaining Medical Works of that Famous and Renowned Physician Dr Thomas Willis*, London: T. Dring, C. Harper, J. Leigh and S. Martyn; facsimile edition ed. William Feindel (1965), Montreal: McGill University Press.

Wilson, C. (1988), 'Visual surface and visual symbol: the microscope and the occult in early modern science', *Journal of the History of Ideas*, xlix (1): 85-108.

Wimsatt, W. K. Jr (1948), *Philosophic Words: A Study of Style and Meaning in the 'Rambler' and 'Dictionary' of Samuel Johnson'*, Yale: University Press; rep. 1968, n. p., Archon Books.

Winograd, T. (1980), 'What does it mean to understand language?', *Cognitive Science* 4: 209-41.

Winstanley, G. (1652), *The Law of Freedom*, in G. H. Sabine (ed.) (1941), *The Works of Gerrard Winstanley*, Ithaca: Cornell University Press.

Wittgenstein, L. (1953), *Philosophical Investigations*, Oxford: Basil Blackwell.

Wynn, T. (1979), 'The intelligence of Late Acheulean hominids', *Man* 14 (N.S.): 371-91.

——(1981), 'The intelligence of Oldowan hominids', *Journal of Human Evolution* 10: 529-41.

Yates, Frances A. (1964), *Giordano Bruno and the Hermetic Tradition*, London: Routledge & Kegan Paul.

Yonge, Charlotte M. (1863), *History of Christian Names*, London: Parker, Son and Bourn.

NAME INDEX

Adam 6
Aesop 52
Allegro, J. 127
Allott, R. 113
Allport, G.W. 11
Apel, K.O. 98
Aristotle 156n
Attar, F.U.-D. 66
Augustine, St 78
Austin, J. 9, 11, 33, 37, 40

Bakan, D. 86
Bean, S.B. 153n
Beck, B.E.E. 69, 156n
Beethoven, L. 97
Benjamin, A.E. 154n
Bennington, G. 76
Berkeley, G. 56
Blumenberg, B. 104
Bornemann, E. 59, 156n
Boucé, P.-G. 154n, 156n
Brainerd, C.J. 58
Brentano, F. 86
Brewer, E.C. 152n
Bromley, D.B. 11
Brown, C.H. 19, 23
Browne, P. 16
Budge, E.A.W. 152n
Bunsen, Baron 11
Bunyan, J. 80
Burton, R. 74, 80

Caesar, J. 97
Campbell, D.T. 146
Campbell, J. 62, 119, 121
Cavendish, H. 82
Chaucer, G. 66
Christ 62

Collins, A.M. 99
Comte, A. 2
Conkey, M.W. 156n
Corman, R. 84
Costall, A. 150n
Coulomb, C.A. 82
Crook, J. 131

Danziger, K. 81
Darwin, C. 2, 3, 103
Davies, T. 45, 75
De Saussure, F. 12
Descartes, R. 73, 74, 77, 78
Desmond, A. 19
Douglas, M. 127
Durkheim, E. 128, 151n

Ehrenreich, B. 155n
Eibl-Eibesfeldt, I. 100
Einstein, A. 94, 95
Eliade, M. 128
Ellen, R.F. 21, 24–7, 29, 30, 151n
Emerson, R.W. 88
English, D. 155n
Erikson, E. 59
Evans-Pritchard, E. 4
Eysenck, H.J. 85

Farrington, B. 68
Fernandez, J. 123–4
Flew, A. 16
Fox, R. 115
Franklin, B. 81
Frazer, J. 128
French, R.K. 81
Freud, S. 74, 85–90, 102, 133

Galileo, G. 77

165

SUBJECT INDEX